LOQUACITIES

LOQUACITIES

CHARLES MACOMB FLANDRAU

Essay Index Reprint Series

BOOKS FOR LIBRARIES PRESS

FREEPORT, NEW YORK

First Published 1931
Reprinted 1968

LIBRARY OF CONGRESS CATALOG CARD NUMBER:

68-22912

PRINTED IN THE UNITED STATES OF AMERICA

To

JAMES AND SOPHIE GRAY

CONTENTS

THE BUSTLE

AN EPISODE OF THE EIGHTIES

"It might be in the attic," I suggested, "although I don't know exactly where."

No one has ever returned from our attic empty-handed, but it is almost equally true that no one ever brings back what he originally went up to find, and Clark that afternoon proved no exception.

"I didn't seem to come across it," he explained when he reappeared at the end of half an hour, "but I did bring down this thing, because I can't make out what it could have been used for," he added as he deposited on my lap an oddly shaped construction of steel wire. "It looks something like a baseball mask, but of course it isn't. At first I thought it might be part of a bird-cage, but the wires are too far apart; the birds would get out. What is it?"

Tenderly, affectionately, sentimentally, I held the strange object in my hands and audibly sighed.

1

"Yes," I answered, "I do know what it is. It's a bustle."

"A bustle?" Clark repeated on a puzzled, a mystified note. "What on earth is a bustle? I never heard of one." With a sudden overpowering sense of time's onward rush, I realized that although he was more than thirty years old, bustles had come and bustles had gone even before he had been born.

"A bustle," I began—but even as I did so, I felt that to one of Clark's generation, whose brief and infrequent excursions into literature concern themselves strictly with the contemporaneous, my attempt to define a bustle would be scarcely more intelligible than a learned antiquarian's discourse on a suit of mediaeval armour.

"But I can't see why they did it," he protested when I had finished. "Take my wife, for instance—she's actually been starving herself for months and tiring herself out with long walks nearly every day because she's so afraid of, well, you know, sticking out behind," he reticently explained. "The one thing she dreads more than sticking out in front is sticking out behind. But

2

those people" (and "those people," as he said it, sounded like something overheard in a museum of Etruscan or Egyptian remains), "those people must have wanted to. Why?"

"Yes, incredible as it may seem to you, they distinctly wanted to," I agreed; "but I can't undertake to make it clear to you (not today anyhow) why the ideal has so entirely changed— gone to the other extreme. That's a job for a historian—a historian with a talent for the philosophy of aesthetics."

"But didn't they look terribly funny with that great, bulbous wire basket hanging on to them under their skirts? Didn't you nearly die laughing?" Clark persisted.

"No—not in the least," I somewhat snappishly told him. "There didn't seem to be anything funny about it. The only women who looked funny in those days were the very few women in town who didn't wear them"; and I recalled the several well-known ladies who simply never indulged in bustles and were always explained and condoned by the fact that they were profoundly intellectual. One, I remember, was a

3

school-teacher who read Sanskrit and Greek for relaxation, and another was a Unitarian who corresponded with Ralph Waldo Emerson. Among their high thoughts the bustle did not mingle.

Clark at length left me with the platitudinous declaration that he had long considered it a waste of time to try to understand women anyhow, and for an hour I reverted to matters in which he had not and never could have a share, but which to me were as vivid and as recent as if they had happened during the past week instead of rather unbelievably far back in the past century.

Queer, queer, I mused, this wire contraption on my lap has become nothing but a ridiculous—a grotesque—relic; yet it was once (and not really so long ago) of supreme importance. It was, all in all, the most ubiquitous feature of the landscape. In my childhood it had the universality that nowadays is exemplified only by the automobile. In a city of three hundred thousand inhabitants it may be that today this is actually the only bustle left. One's ideal of female loveliness was unquestionably akin to that of the Hottentot; but in the eighteen eighties it was a fact that without a bustle female loveliness simply did not—could not—exist. It was pre-eminently an era of gelatinous convexities, and women, unfortunate in having been by the Creator scantily upholstered half-way down behind and rather high up in front, resorted without scruple to the medium of art. The bustle and the "form improver" moulded not only anatomies, but entire lives; they determined female fates—changed destinies. In my hearing at an early age a young man passionately declared that he had decided never to propose to a certain girl because, as he delicately expressed it, "I think, by God, that there's deception in that bust." More often than not the size and set of a bustle was an index of character—a barometer of morals. Mrs. Bates, the wife of a major stationed at the Fort, always wore a conspicuously, an astoundingly, large one. It shot out abruptly, even violently, from the base of her spine like a shelf (without the slightest danger one could have stood a glass of water or a plate of soup on it) and then, in a long, dashing, thrilling curve, swooped all the way down to the ground and about two feet beyond. Hers was a challenging, a defiant, a brazen bustle.

"I like Mrs. Bates," I once announced when at the end of an afternoon call she had rattled away to the Fort in the shabby old leather ambulance drawn by four fiends in the guise of mules.

"She may be a kind-hearted woman," my maiden aunt grudgingly conceded with sudden thin, straight lips, "but she's fast. Look at her bustle." The bustle, too, served on occasions as a kind of ambulatory show case or exhibition grounds. At the annual charity ball, for instance, for women of a certain age a projecting, overhanging, black-velvet backside draped like a mantelpiece or a bureau with little lambrequins of one's most expensive lace was almost obligatory—a kind of dress uniform. And, as they were the fashion, enormously fat women as a matter of course wore them quite as universally as did the thin ones.

"When a woman built like Mrs. Gilman ties a bustle to herself," my father once declared

6

at the dinner-table, "it's like piling Pelion on—on—"

"On Assa," my half brother brilliantly interposed. At which my mother, with wholly unconvincing severity, ordered him to leave the table and the room and not come back.

I hadn't forgotten these far-off things, but for years I hadn't thought of them, and as I sat there, I went on to remember the hectic, the historical and hysterical autumn evening when, while my father was reading the *Dispatch* in the library after dinner, he suddenly looked up and demanded that morning's *Pioneer Press*. In the *Dispatch* he had come across a somewhat vague and sketchy reference to something (a lawsuit, no doubt) that in the morning paper had been treated of at length, but which, in the hurry of getting to the courthouse in time, had escaped his eye. As usual, he was in his big chair at one side of the library table; I was at its farther end, sitting on the ledge of the bookcase, trying to "do" my arithmetic for the following day. Mother was leaning back in a rocking-chair near the fire. In the dining-room, across the hall,

Aunt Dottie and my half brother, John, were playing backgammon while grandmother, under the cast-iron dining-room chandelier, which held six kerosene lamps (there were in the house thirty-six kerosene lamps, every one of which had to be cleaned and refilled every day), was crocheting purple scallops on a fluffy, white, knitted thing, known in those days as "a cloud."

"The *Pioneer Press*?" echoed my mother. "I'll get it for you. It's probably in the kitchen." But, most tediously, the *Pioneer Press* wasn't in the kitchen, and it wasn't in any of the three kitchen pantries. Furthermore, it couldn't be found in the dining-room or the parlour or any of the family's five bedrooms.

"Are Mary Egan and Jane Munson at home?" roared my father at the foot of the stairs. "They've probably burned it," he added with bitterness. He was not a patient person, and, like almost everyone else in the world, his patience was peculiarly, acutely tried—stretched to the breaking-point—when he had made up his mind instantly to read something—anything—

8

that turned out to be mislaid, or burned, or pur-
loined.

"Ask those girls what they did with it," he
shouted.

Miraculously, Mary Egan, who originally had
been my nurse, and who now was the waitress,
and Jane Munson, who had long been our cook,
were at home. As a rule they went to a dance
every night except Sunday, swathed respectively
in uncountable yards of blue and pink tarlatan
and asphyxiatingly calcimined with a delirious
mauve liquid that came in a bottle labelled
"Laird's Bloom of Youth." But of the *Pioneer
Press* Mary and Jane, who were in their room,
repairing the havoc wrought by the feet of fire-
men at the dance of the night before, knew nothing. They couldn't have burned it, they pointed
out, as the kitchen stove had been functioning
for hours before my father came downstairs and
as usual read the thing at breakfast, and the library fire had been laid for several days without
being lighted.

"But I want it," my father insisted. "I want
to read something in it—something of impor-

tance. If it hasn't been destroyed, it must be in the house. I don't suppose it just jumped off the dining-room table where I left it and strolled out of the front door."

"I can't imagine," began my mother. "I can't imagine," she repeated in a moment, but in a tone of noticeably less conviction. And then she suddenly sat down in the rocking-chair and by turning her back and frantically poking the fire, which didn't need poking, tried to conceal the fact that she had become feeble with laughter. But naturally my father caught her at it and, with the elaborate and glacial politeness that is ever the signal of suppressed rage, he said: "Really, my dear, I can't quite see what is so excruciating in the fact that I am being extremely annoyed."

"It's because—it's because it has all at once come over me that I know where it is," mother finally managed to gasp. She had given up and broken down completely.

"You know where it is?" father thundered. "Then why don't you get it for me—or at least tell me where it is and let me get it."

"Oh, no—no," mother protested with something that was a cross between a sob and a moan. "You couldn't possibly get it. You couldn't."

"If it wouldn't be too much trouble, will you kindly explain why not?" father then acidly inquired.

"You couldn't get it—you couldn't get it because—mother—is wearing—it," she then heroically brought out.

"Your mother, Mrs. McClure, is wearing a newspaper? How on earth can a woman wear a newspaper? Where is she wearing it?" father, in angry amazement, demanded.

"Oh, don't—don't," mother pleaded. "I can't in so many words tell you where she wears them, but with your legal brain," she wildly added, "I think you ought to be able to make a more or less accurate deduction. She wears them for bustles."

"Mrs. McClure uses the *Pioneer Press* for a bustle?" father hissed. "Oh, my God," he muttered as he clutched the arms of his chair and rolled his eyes. "Why, why, with the whole world filled to overflowing—teeming—positively

11

bursting with potential bustle material, does she deliberately, wilfully, perversely choose the *Pioneer Press*—my *Pioneer Press?*"

"It's more economical," mother, having partly got control of herself, tried to explain. "And then, too, she's afraid of the wire ones—she doesn't trust them. After they've been worn a long time, they have been known to collapse and run into people's—and run into people. A *Pioneer Press* folded over a piece of tape and tied around the waist is perfectly safe. Sometimes, of course, it does get loose and fall off in the street, but she just kicks it aside and walks on, pretending it wasn't hers."

"But I want it—I want it right away," father wailed. "I realize, naturally, that I can't get it myself," he admitted with an attempt at sweet reasonableness, "but you can."

"But I won't," replied mother with spirit and decision. "I absolutely refuse to ask her to undress at eight o'clock in the evening merely because you have an uncontrollable desire—an uncontrollable desire to read her bustle. I think it's indecent."

More nearly like what is known as a "scene"
than anything my parents had—before me at
least—ever indulged in, the atmosphere of the library for the next few moments was nervous,
disconcerting, slightly poisonous. Father spas-
modically drummed on the arms of his chair with
his fingers, and in a kind of atavistic French
fashion nervously shrugged and made faces.
Mother violently rocked and, from time to time,
once more overcome, leaned far forward and
poked the fire.

"Well, anyhow, she does go to bed at ten
o'clock," he at last hopefully reflected.

"Yes—usually," mother agreed, but with considerably less optimism.

"You can get it then, can't you?" he asked.

"Oh, yes, I can get it then. I'll slip into her
room, but after she's asleep, of course. It would
upset her dreadfully if she knew."

That evening, however, "then," for some unaccountable reason, appeared to have determined
never to arrive. It tarried, lingered, hesitated,
changed its mind, got its second wind, and took a
fresh hold. Nine o'clock struck, half past nine,

and finally ten, at which father, bounding from his chair as if propelled by some hidden mechanism, began both ostentatiously and deafeningly to lock up. He pulled down heavy windows with a perilous bang, smashed the inside shutters together till everyone jumped, opened the front door, slammed it shut again, and then went back and did it a second time. He then blew out the lamps in the parlour and the hall and, standing in the dining-room doorway, exclaimed to grandmother, with a kind of hollow heartiness (she was now alone there): "Well—I don't know what you're going to do, but I'm going to bed."

"Are you?" murmured grandmother with no interest whatever—not even glancing up from her purple scallops. "I should if I were you. You can put out these lights—I can't reach them —and I'll go into the library. Finishing a piece of work like this always seems to excite me a little."

The hours from eight to ten had been merely so much time—a long time to be sure, but, after all, just time. From ten to one A.M., however,

14

was pure, abstract, metaphysical, Einsteinian eternity, with a kind of beginning, perhaps, but with no predictable end. Father, after prolonged, undertoned, sepulchral urging, consented to undress, but refused to lie down or, for more than a minute or two, to sit down. In that most humorous of all human coverings, a nightshirt, he drifted interminably back and forth in the upper hall, scared me almost into screams by now and then suddenly sitting on the edge of my bed just as I was falling asleep, and creaked up and down the front stairs and past the library door four different times. The first three of these expeditions were productive of a single, reiterated, cryptic, intensely bitter phrase. Thrusting his head into the twilight of mother's room, he would mutter: "Still sitting on it," and then resume his restless promenade. Before his fourth descent, however, grandmother herself creaked up the stairs, went to her room, apparently found something she wanted, and, just as we had begun to feel that she had come up for the night, creaked out and down again. This time when father returned from below he no longer re-

15

ported "Still sitting on it," but: "She's begun on solitaire."

I seem to have fallen asleep about then, and some time between one in the morning and breakfast mother of course rescued what remained of the *Pioneer Press* and provided a perfectly good substitute, but all the next day was a most dreadful day, for when cheerful, energetic, sparkling grandmother appeared at breakfast, she was another creature—a changed woman. She scarcely spoke, sighed a great deal, and, listlessly protesting that she was perfectly well, left the table after having sipped a quarter of a cup of tea. From the garden, where she went to do a little weeding among the asters and dahlias, she, who had never in her life been tired, returned in less than half an hour in a state of complete exhaustion, and by noon she had thrown the household into an almost tearful panic by going upstairs and actually lying down. My mother and my aunt had whispered consultations behind locked doors. Two earnest apprehensive communications were written to the family doctor, almost sent, and then torn up, and from noon till eve our world was enveloped in a kind of solemn, melancholy hush. Throughout the afternoon mother was tenderly solicitous (no one could have been more so), but, as I hovered in the background of grandmother's bedroom, I seemed, from time to time, to detect in her voice a note of something almost like impatience—even of exasperation. For grandmother refused to admit a pain, an ache, a chill, or a temperature of any kind and looked, as she always did, rosy, pretty, and extremely solid.

And then, at last, I heard her say rather tremulously: "Yes, something did happen—a dreadful thing. It was bound to come sooner or later —I've always known that, of course—but I didn't think it could come overnight. It has, though. Rebecca, I'm an old, old woman."

"But what utter nonsense!" mother protested. "People in perfect health simply don't get old right off like that. What in the world makes you imagine you have?"

"I don't exactly like to tell you," grandmother hesitated, "because you're far too young really to understand; but this morning while I was dressing, I remembered that when I was making my bustle yesterday, I had noticed under 'Household Hints' a recipe for getting rid of mice in a pleasant, friendly way that they enjoy. Of course there aren't any mice, but you never can tell, and I meant to cut it out, and then, when I unfolded my bustle and began to look, it wasn't the *Pioneer Press* at all. It was last night's *Dispatch*.

"Yes, yes, but what of it?" mother urged her on.

"I knew you couldn't understand," grandmother sighed. "What happened was that I must have got up during the night, gone all the way downstairs, found the *Dispatch*, and made a new bustle; but the awful part of it is that I have no recollection of doing anything of the kind. From the time I went to bed, my mind was a perfect blank. I must have put the first bustle—the *Pioneer Press*—away somewhere, because I haven't been able to find it; but I can't remember even that. Rebecca, I am breaking up."

It was gay, I remembered, to see grandmother a moment or two later suddenly snap back from

18

a self-imposed senility to a youthful middle age—
—not unlike being present when a locust leaves
its shell on a fence, or a butterfly pops out of a
cocoon. And I remembered, too, that the next
day mother subscribed to the Butler, Pennsylvania, *Clarion Herald,* which nobody in the family ever by any chance wanted to read, and which
grandmother wore undisturbed to the last.

MEMORY AND MRS. GRINDER

RECENTLY, and with a definite object in view, I sweated through an obese work that dealt with the subject of "memory and imagination." My object was to find out if possible what became of a thought when you were no longer thinking it. Where does it retire to? What does it do with itself in the meanwhile? It must have some sort of existence, because if it didn't, it could never return, and of course thoughts of every possible description continually do return, sometimes after long intervals. It would be interesting, I felt, to learn what theories had been advanced as to the nature of memory. Was it, for instance, continuous? That is to say, does every thought a person has keep going on like a stream of water until it is at last turned off by death, or does it scuttle into some sort of a compartment or pigeon-hole and remain there until an external influence disturbs it and routs it out into renewed activity? The volume I consulted seemed to treat of this matter exhaustively and

20

with authority, but as far as I was concerned, the explanation was a total loss. In order to get much out of it you had to be on desperate terms of intimacy with expressions like "dichotomy" and "absolute indeterminism," "psychophysical parallelism," "heliotropic," "plumule," "colloids," "epiphenomenal," and "ideational continuum."

This being the case, I was forced to abandon the hope of ever knowing where my thought of Mrs. Grinder has been during, literally, the thirty-five years that have passed since I last thought of her. Thirty-five years ago, and for some years before that, I used to hear and think about Mrs. Grinder a great deal. Then she passed out of my mind and stayed out of it until, one afternoon in New England, a few months ago, she suddenly and horribly came back to it again. Where she had been during more than a quarter of a century I have been unable to discover, but when just the right combination of circumstances presented themselves, she vividly returned.

In the early and middle part of the last century Mrs. Grinder lived somewhere in Pennsylvania. My family knew her slightly and regarded her as a gentle, deeply religious woman with the sweet smile and grey hair of sainted motherhood. Mrs. Grinder travelled a good deal. She did not go very far, but she went frequently, and no doubt she gave plausible reasons for her periodic absences from home, because for a long time it did not occur to anybody to question them. Then, with unfeeling abruptness, it did. A perfectly healthy child to whom Mrs. Grinder had, on a railway train, affectionately given a slice of cake became acutely ill and died in its mother's arms before the train reached the next station. Mrs. Grinder somehow had slipped up; she had been careless. The children to whom she had all along made a practice of giving cake on her excursions throughout the state of Pennsylvania had never become sick and died before, until she had had a chance to get off the train and take another going somewhere else. Mrs. Grinder's diversion had been, not to see them die, but to go home and think about it—gloat over it. On this final occasion, however, she had either

22

baked too large a dose in the cake, or the object of her benefaction was unusually frail. Anyhow she was arrested; an incredible number of sorrowing parents all over the state remembered her perfectly, and the dear lady's trips on railway trains ceased for all time. One thing in connexion with her that obstinately refuses to come back again into my mind is whether or not Mrs. Grinder was hanged. But do let us hope for the worst.

Now, while my early education by no means began and ended with this fascinating pathological memoir, the story of Mrs. Grinder, it must be confessed, loomed large in it. It was valuable both as a dramatic narrative that, as told by one's grandmother (who had once actually lived within a few doors of the Grinder home), never lost its gruesome thrill, and also as an awful, bloodcurdling warning to little boys never under any circumstances to eat from the hand of a stranger. Doubtless all children are deeply impressed by some one or two details of their teaching to the exclusion of others perhaps more important. Never shall I forget the lonely-looking

23

American child in an upper corridor of a Parisian
hotel who once called out to me (aged eight)
and my brother (aged four): "I'm so sorry I
can't play with you. My mother is afraid you
may have a disease!"

At any rate, until the age of ten or eleven Mrs.
Grinder would have a prominent page should I
ever write a pamphlet entitled "Women Who
Have Influenced Me"; and then suddenly for
thirty-five years I forgot all about her.

It was on an indescribably hot afternoon in a
Pullman car that last summer she came back to
me. In the section opposite was a benevolent-
looking woman with a male child of about four,
and even if the child hadn't spent most of the
afternoon in falling down, hurting itself, and
howling as it galloped from one end of the aisle
to the other, it would have been impossible to
remain unaware of mother and son for long, as
the woman was almost completely deaf. The
child's voice had of necessity become a piercing
scream. Passengers who were trying to read or
take a nap simply had to haul down the flag and
surrender. I tried to get into the half dressing-

room, half smoking-compartment at the end of
the car, but the same happy idea, for the same
unhappy reason, had occurred to nine other men
before I acted upon it. Rather than go back,
three of them sat for almost two hours in the tin
wash-basins, and when I sought refuge among
them, there wasn't any room. Then in a fatal
moment of something—kind-heartedness, hy-
pocrisy, or a sort of imbecile weakness brought
on by physical and mental exhaustion—I don't
know what it was—I caught the child's tearful
eye and smiled. It was but a faint, fleeting smile,
but it was by far the most irreparably successful
one that my visage had ever indulged in, for it
both sealed my fate and spelled my doom. In
much less time than it takes to write it, the child
was across the aisle in the seat beside me and, with
the briefest preliminary pawing, and tugging at
my necktie by way of introduction, on my lap
with a strangle hold around my neck. The ther-
mometer was registering all of ninety-four degrees, the dust had been suffocating ever since
the train had started, almost visible waves of dis-
comfort and impatience and ill temper had em-

anated from everybody in the car, and even now
I cannot with calmness describe the half-hour
that followed.

Radiant that the charm of her offspring had at
last made itself felt, the mother leaned forward
and, in the strange loud voice of persons who for
many years have been unable to hear themselves
speak, declared: "You love children, don't you?
Somehow I can always tell." With mental reservations to the effect that I was fonder of them
sometimes than I was at other times, I truthfully
replied that I liked them very much, but of
course she didn't understand me. She insisted on
my repeating what I had said several times, and
as I struggled like a mariner in the clutches of a
giant octopus to disengage her infant son's sticky
hands from the back of my neck and screamed
three times that yes, I did like children, I became
aware that the passengers had one and all shaken
off their weariness and apathy and were beginning to enjoy themselves. Our subsequent conversation I prefer to pass over hurriedly. I can
still see myself pulling the child's hand out of my
mouth and keeping it out long enough to yell,

26

as if I were trying to communicate with someone
at the other end of a ten-acre lot, that no, I
hadn't any of my own—no, I wasn't married—
no, I wasn't even engaged. And all of these
sacred disclosures, and many more, had to be
shrieked out, not only once, but twice and often
thrice. There was no evading her. "What did
you say? Say it again, please, I don't hear very
well." And then, without warning, came the
incident of the blueberry pie. The woman
opened a basket on the seat in front of her and
took out a large plate on which, drowning in its
own sickly purple juice and already cut into tri-
angles of more or less equal dimensions, was a
blotchy-looking blueberry pie. The child let go
of me, lifted its fat perspiring bulk from my
chest, slid to the floor, and, crossing over to its
mother, received two exuding slabs—one for itself "and one for the nice gentleman." Whereupon I recalled the fact that somebody had once
strongly advised the patient Job to curse God and
die. I also, for the first time in thirty-five years,
remembered every ghastly detail of my grandmother's personal recollections of Mrs. Grinder

27

and I resolved that, although the mother and her child had between them managed to hypnotize me into taking their wet pie in my hand, no power on earth could compel me to taste it. The fact that it had been cut into sections beforehand was conclusive proof that the piece she had given her babe was harmless, and that the one she had so carefully chosen for me was a combination of strychnine, arsenic, and bichloride of mercury. Never in my life have I felt more firm than I did at that moment. I had no idea of what to do with the thing; I only knew I wasn't going to eat it. When it began to dribble through my fingers on my white flannel trousers, I calmly opened a copy of *Scribner's* magazine and let it drip all over an instalment of a story by Edith Wharton.

"Mamma—the gentleman isn't eating it," the child would complain, in a voice that could have been heard by the passing vessels on Long Island Sound.

"Oh, but he will, deary. Just you wait and see," mamma would megaphone back. And at last, when the whole carful was tense with excitement over just what I was going to do with it, I jumped up and with the clammy mess in my hand bolted for the door. Half-way down the aisle the revolting instrument of death broke and fell on the floor with a dark, bluish-purple splash, but I didn't stop to pick it up. I found the porter asleep in the car ahead, and, rousing him from his slumber, I told him to be very careful when he went back not to step on something in the middle of the aisle, and above all not to eat it. I myself never went back. Instead I found a seat in the smoking-car about a mile and a half farther on and spent the rest of the day in considering the nature of memory.

Since my grandmother had last told me about Mrs. Grinder and since I had last thought of her, people had been born in the world, grown up, and in turn become mothers and even grandmothers themselves. Grandmothers of thirty-five are by no means unusual. It is possible that in all that time Mrs. Grinder had never once been thought of by anybody. Where, during the long interval, had she been secluded? What was the nature of her continued existence? For she came back into my consciousness with all the reality of a wax murderess in the chamber of horrors. Mrs. Grinder was just a memory, but what, I should greatly like to know, is just a memory?

YELLOWED WITH AGE

THERE are letters and old letters and letters "yellowed with age." Letters—just letters—the patient postman distributes several times a day; old letters are letters written by persons one loved who have since died, or by persons one cared for and with whom one has quarrelled or from whom one has "drifted apart." But while one may or may not have heard of the writers of letters that have become yellowed with age, one never knew them or saw them; it all happened too long ago for that. Letters that are merely old are usually sad, by which, of course, I mean that one is sad when one reads them. But sad as it is in their power to make me, I do not find them in themselves interesting. Having lived through that to which they refer, one always knows infinitely more than they reveal. As tangible souvenirs they may be precious, but as reading-matter they are rather pathetically out of date, like bodices with puffed sleeves, or "tournures," or one's own photograph at the age of twenty-six. Merely

31

old letters have ceased to be news without having become information.

Quite different, however, are the four neat packets I have just restored to their battered little sepulchre of unpainted tin. For although to the eye they are of a greyish whiteness, to the mind or perhaps the heart—they are, in the sacred phrase of English literature, "all yellowed with age."

Often as I have read the forty-five letters they contain I have wondered why I, who am so little concerned in the affairs of my neighbours, should always be so absorbed and moved by the daily lives of four obscure Irish people who wrote long, rambling, and, according to current ideas, stilted letters a hundred and thirty-one years ago. It is true they were written by my great-great-grandfather and grandmother, their daughter Mary, and their son John, to Tom (another son—my great-grandfather), then a boy of seventeen who had left Dublin and was seeking his fortune in the law office of one of the numerous Biddles of Philadelphia. But to a twentieth-century American the immediate family circle of one's great-great-grandfather is sentimentally, after all, rather remote and I doubt if it would have long continued to interest me if the letters did not, quite unconsciously, tell a coherent little story—if they did not leave upon one the impression as of an artless little work of art. In reading them I have had sudden flashes of insight into why certain works of fiction are literature and others are not. The letters do not happen to be fiction, although after more than a century and a quarter they might just as well be, but they are literature. For with due attention to technique, which in their case is the epistolary style of the time, they transcribe something of life into words; life, not as it might be or ought to be, but as it was and is. There is ambition and hope and courage, deep love and great faith in these letters, but there is also disappointment, suspicion, bitterness, tragedy, and grief, as there is in almost every life, however small a part it plays on however small a stage.

Possibly there are families in this world over which the dove of peace has perpetually hovered, but my own has never been one of them. My childhood, I recall, was at frequent intervals dramatic with overheard references to half a dozen members of the family whose names (theoretically "never mentioned") were, in reality, colloquial eponyms of the perfidious and immoral. Some of these cloven-hoofed personalities we had wilfully, madly married, and them it was always in order—even a kind of etiquette—conversationally to break on the wheel, flay, quarter, and boil in oil. But there were others that we had simply and inadvertently begot ourselves— domestic rather than imported devils—and they, I remember, were usually alluded to not so much in anger as in sorrow.

Apparently our collection of family fiends in human form was quite as complete in the eighteenth century as it seemed to be during most of the nineteenth, for the letters of Mr. and Mrs. Collins, Mary, and John to Thomas, Jr., in faraway Philadelphia fairly bristle with references to them—references that from time to time become apprehensive warnings.

"J. C——, son of your uncle Robert, will bring you a letter from your father which he could not avoid giving, but desired me to give you a caution not to engage your reputation for him as he has been a very idle, unsettled lad," John remarks in a letter to brother Tom in 1793, adding: "However, if you can serve him in any manner without running a risk, you will serve your family." And in regard to this same prospective undesirable citizen of the United States Mary at about the same time cautions her elder brother: "I hope your acquaintance with J. C—— may be as distant as possible, for be assured that neither his disposition nor his principles are such as entitle him to your friendship, however sincere they may appear to you." Mr. Collins, while disapproving of the idle and unsettled J. C—— did not consider him entirely hopeless as he suggests that if the young man "could be given a military career, he might possibly acquit himself." Compared to some of the others, however, J. C—— was really harmless.

"It is the most earnest request I ever made, nay even prayer, that, let the event be what it may, you will not have the smallest acquaintance with anyone of your name in America except James," the old gentleman writes; a comprehensive entreaty in which Mary, in a letter that went by the same ship (ironically named the *Olive Branch*) throws a specific light by informing Tom that:

"Phillip N——, the attorney who served under either Emor or Roger N——, I don't know which, has been in Newgate for a shocking forgery. I do not know the particulars of the transaction but I tell it to you as I hear. He is going to Philadelphia as he has had a very narrow escape of being hanged or transported. I think it would have been happy for his relatives if he had. I hope you will guard against knowing him if he goes there, as it must ruin your connections for life to know such a person though he is only a third cousin to you." Even my great-great-grandmother, gentle, affectionate, religious, and rheumatic as the letters which extend over a period of twenty-four years prove her to have been, always had a sudden wild Irish gleam in her near-sighted eyes when she wrote of her relatives.

"What you mention about that most infamous

of all villains, Edward C——, has very much damped my joy," she declares in 1794. And again:

"Your cousin Cliff lives with your Uncle Ford and pays two guineas per week. He has been repeatedly within two minutes' walk of us but never thought proper to ask how your father was until the other day when he knew he would shortly leave here."

"As to the relations you inquire about," she answers on another occasion, "I shall not waste time and paper for so very worthless a tribe."

"All our *friends* everywhere are well. Don't mistake me—I did not say relations," writes Mary with a bitterness I at first thought was excessive. There is, in fact, a note of acerbity and youthful pessimism in all of Mary's earlier letters from Dublin, the reason for which did not dawn on me until I had read them several times. But when finally I understood it, the young girl's attitude for the moment towards life in general seemed more than justified, for apparently, owing to the machinations of one of the devils (a cousin), Mr. Collins had lost

37

a flourishing business (he had been a linen-draper), had gone bankrupt, and was, in 1790, when the letters begin, sojourning with his wife and son and daughter in a debtor's prison. Not that any of them ever actually mention the fact in so many words, although Tom, of course, knew of it, as the calamity had happened before he left Ireland.

"I am under the disagreeable necessity of informing my dearest child that I am still in the same odious situation as when we parted," Mr. Collins delicately remarks in his first communication:

"Your father at present remains in the same embarrassing position but is, however, flattered with the hopes of a speedy extrication," is one of John's references to the subject.

"A sufficient Providence and our great and merciful God continue to give us all good health, but our spirits are very much depressed at being still in this horrid place," sighs Mrs. Collins.

"You know of your father's trying predicament," writes Mary. "Therefore it would be needless for me to say anything of it to you as

38

I am sure your own feelings will paint this dreadful place much better than it is possible for me." The term "debtor's prison" is never employed, but even while I understand this reticence and applaud the general disinclination to offend Tom with painful details, I greatly regret the evasion of them. Beyond being "odious" and "embarrassing," "trying," "dreadful," and "horrid" I have always longed to know in what their life in prison consisted. How many rooms did they have? Where and what did they eat? Did they indulge in "light housekeeping" or was there for the inmates a sort of refectory? Mother and children could come and go as they pleased, for John, one learns, "is very well settled in a business house in Dame Street at a tolerably handsome salary," and Mary now and then "spent a week at the Rock with Mrs. Williams," or "drank tea with her cousin Betty North." But was Mr. Collins permitted to leave the premises? The style of their letters and the frequent references to books, music, and pictures show them to have been persons, not only of education, but of cultivated tastes. While in prison how did

39

they employ their time? All of Mary's usual occupations had inevitably ceased. "I am very sensible of the loss I suffered when deprived of my harpsichord, but I do not repine at it," she says, although she "deplores" the necessity of giving up her "writing master," whose services they could not longer afford. In almost every letter she apologizes to her clever and polished older brother for the consequent deterioration of her handwriting. Later on, after her father had been happily "extricated," one rejoices to read that the interrupted pursuits were resumed.

"Your wishes respecting our sister's writing have been long since fulfilled," says John a year and a half later, "and I hope that her present letters will convince you that the want of a writing master has been supplied by one of the best in town. As for the rest of her education, we have procured her a spinnet, to which she pays an uncommon attention, having much improved her former knowledge without assistance. In the article of reading, I have been able to supply her tolerably well with history, poetry and Belles Lettres. This I have always done and

will continue to do in compliance with your
wishes. When our affairs assume a more competent aspect she shall be supplied with proper
masters for the completion of her education."
During the period of the "trying predicament,"
however, time in "this stupid, empty Dublin,"
as Mary calls the place, must have dragged
wearily for the young girl, and worse than her
enforced idleness was the constant sense of hu-
miliation.

"I have not seen any of Mrs. Whitmore's family for some months as I do not like to go anywhere without making a return, and was it in
my power, I could not expect any of them to
come here," she declares, adding: "Mrs. Whitmore came to bring me to the Rock the last time
I was there; but she was so much shocked at
coming into this place that we could not expect
she would come again." Poor little proud, sensitive, sixteen-year-old Mary—it is not to be
wondered at that her letters during this time invariably contain lugubrious items and reflections
like the following:

"I am sorry to inform you that dear Mrs. Dillon was taken from her unhappy family by a fever, and the cruelty of the sheriff's men was such that they had her carried to the hall door and kept her there with all the family while they took legal possession of the house and concerns, and I am sorry to add that Mr. Dillon does not feel so much for her loss as might be expected, but it is impossible to know anyone in this world and I think they are supremely happy that are out of it, if we could expect to be deserving of a better fate than is met with here.

Happy state in which the dead are cast,
Their pain is gone, their pleasures past!

On the 29th of July, 1791, however, Mr. Collins was able to write his son the glad news that "At last I am, thanks be to God, a perfectly free man as my creditors have accepted of an assignment of a property and have given me a general discharge," and it is agreeable to note how immediate and cheering was the effect of this event on the family spirits. Mr. Collins at once became enthusiastic over half a dozen small business

42

prospects, any one of which appeared to him in the light of a modest gold mine that, as he usually expresses it, would "afford ample provision for those to whom an all wise and omnipotent Creator may vouchsafe an existence protracted beyond the limits of my own earthly sojourn."

"He is likewise at this present moment soliciting a place under the Grand Canal Company," writes John. "It is called 'Inspectorship of Passage Boats' and worth about 200 per annum. The directors are all sworn to choose the most worthy. Should they adhere closely to that I think he would be chosen, but fearful of anything which might co-operate so as to bias them he has made considerable interest and has received every possible encouragement. This does not prevent him from endeavouring to establish himself in business. However, as he will write to you himself, I shall not say any more of him except that since his enlargement" (delightful word) "he has considerably altered for the better both in appearance and in health." For the moment his "enlargement" entirely changed the tone of his letters, as it did those of all of them, but I have been quite unable to discover that his numerous projects resulted in anything particularly brilliant or lucrative. Neither, it seems, could Tom, whose brains and industry had already begun to make an impression in Mr. Biddle's Philadelphia office. Tom had been in the New World for almost a year and a half now, and, while I have not, of course, any of his letters to his father in Dublin, one instinctively knows what some of them contained, on reading his father's replies. The young man's world was indeed new—a world of new ambitions, methods, and rewards. Until then he had taken Ireland and Dublin and his father for granted, but after a year and a half of Philadelphia it is evident that he began to *see* them, and with the priggish severity of youth he commented on what he saw. Hatred wastes more valuable time than even love does, and Tom was too busy as well as too far away to keep on hating a whole county full of uncles and cousins. He was also greatly bored by his father's incorrigible optimism and frankly said so, for in 1794, in a letter beginning: "My Ever Dearest Tom," and ending with: "I shall

44

say no more than that I am my darling Tom's most affectionate father," Mr. Collins pathetically defends himself.

"In respect to what you say relative to my expectations being unrealized," he replies, "I forgive the heat of some of your expressions as I am sure they arose from your ordeal" (I don't know what the "ordeal" was), "and it is impossible for me at this distance to say more on the subject than to assure you that those expectations are *not* 'visionary' or 'very trifling.' The fact is I thank God that through my own and the exertions of some very sincere friends, I have secured something like a tolerable provision for my family. My intentions are to settle either in your part of the world or in a part of Europe that I shall not at present name." The dear man was perpetually involved in activities he could not "for the moment name" or "disclose," "reveal," or sometimes even "more specifically elucidate." As my great-great-grandfather had every intention of settling either on the continent of America or on the continent of Europe, it was entirely natural and characteristic of him

45

to end up in the West Indies on the island of Dominica.

Until the time of his "enlargement" his letters as well as John's and Mary's are intensely personal, pessimistic, and brief, but with freedom and more "competent" circumstances they at once become chatty volumes of general information, interspersed with solid pages of "fine writing" and highfalutin "reflections" that, in their day, were no doubt valuable and welcome. As letters from my great-great-uncle and aunt to my great-grandfather I find them delightful still, but should my own brothers and sisters suddenly begin to communicate with me in anything remotely resembling the style of these eighteenth-century epistles, I should consider it my trying duty immediately to consult the probate court. Mary, both because her tastes were "literary" and because she was a girl and had more time, indulges in prolonged linguistic orgies on the slightest provocation. Without doubt they were laboriously composed and carefully transcribed from several "foul copies," but in the artificial fashion of the day she invariably

46

apologizes for the careless haste with which she scribbled them, and manages to give the impression that the captain of the *Betsey,* the *Olive Branch,* the *Washington,* or the *Endeavour* is impatiently fuming at her elbow. The following bouquet of rhetorical wax flowers gives some idea of little Mary's epistolary style at its most luxuriant:

"To begin with I should wish you to copy the Frenchman a little more who is always merry and pleased. Don't mistake me, for I think a person incapable of thought degraded to a brute. But look on the smooth surface of a sheet of water, and you will see it calm and unruffled as a morning in May; look to the bottom, however, and you will see storms that only wait for a favourable opportunity to drive away the calm and take its place. Therefore the most pleasing prospect being at the top I would not look deeper for fear of being made gloomy by too much reflection. Yet, if you must think, as every active mind should, lead your thoughts to a more general path; if you must contemplate, let your contemplation be on the divine works of God and the many and innumerable blessings He has bestowed on man.

"I do not coincide entirely in your opinion that the fortitude, good qualities and prudence of any one untried by adversity is at best like untubbed gold, the value of which cannot be estimated. I am more inclined to think with Addison who, when asked his opinion of a person in adversity . . . ." (Here follows a quotation from that expert chef of verbal doughnuts, Joseph Addison.) "I hope that you will agree with me that the surest way of being able to bear the smiles of Fortune is the remembrance of having already borne its frowns with humbleness and, when in our power, to do good universally to all our fellow creatures who are in our reach. But the surest way of regulating our conduct is by copying that divine philosopher Seneca who, when retired to rest, would not admit of good-natured Morpheus shedding his poppies around his head until he had first taken a retrospect of his conduct, actions, words and even thoughts during the day he had past." What a charming original is this to copy!

"I have seen your letter to John and I was very much pleased with the advice it contained concerning the disposition of time, which, I am happy to learn, you set a proper value on. I find you have studied Locke to a good purpose and I hope the next letter you write me shall be filled with a dissertation on Infinity, Expanse, Duration, Simple and Complex Ideas, Time, Space and Truth, Ample Modes, etc. You may from this perceive that I too have read but not studied Locke as I think his writings too abstruse for a weak female and fit only for you sensible men." For a weak female of seventeen, I beg to observe that this is "going some."

But of course the letters by no means consisted solely of purple patches, and the thoughtful detail in which all the news of the day was recorded for Tom's enlightenment causes one to realize with bewildering vividness the comparative unimportance of letter-writing a hundred and some years later. Inevitably one stops reading to consider again the old question of whether what has been gained from telegraph wires and hourly newspapers altogether compensates for what has been lost by having long since outgrown the necessity of thinking, reporting, and editing for ourselves. Ireland then as now and always was seething with religion and politics. The complicated theological and material interests of Catholics and Protestants were clashing with their periodic violence, and, while I have little interest in the controversy itself, Mary's long, and apparently intelligent, analysis of it, and John's more technical summary of the situation, are curiously impressive. The two write from a point of view severely Protestant, but, even so, they at least *had* a point of view in which they were deeply interested. Today a girl of seventeen who in every letter to an adored brother should write from four to eight or ten careful pages on the tariff, the reparations report, or the Government's Japanese policy would quite simply be an intellectual monstrosity. Perversely and morbidly she would be going out of her way to do something that newspapers and periodicals do infinitely quicker and better. But there was nothing unusual or especially intellectual about Mary. She merely happened to live at a time when important, as well as trivial, news was disseminated chiefly by one's family and one's friends. It is one of the easiest things in the world to skip the columns of a newspaper that look solid and serious, to live for months without any clear and definite idea of what, for instance, Congress and the legislature are accomplishing and evading; but constant talk and discussion are not only entertaining in themselves, they are for purely social reasons difficult to elude. Young as John and Mary were, their knowledge of contemporary questions was considerable for the simple reason that they were unable to escape it, and they conscientiously imparted it, together with the local gossip of Dublin, to Tom. Thus in 1791 Tom, in a letter from home, learns that "His Majesty, it is understood, will take part with the Turks in a war they have commenced with the Empress of Russia. The Minister is raising a fleet to go up the Baltic Sea to join the Turks this summer, as we are anxious to have the proud Catherine humbled. I am sorry to tell you that Mrs. FitzGerald died sometime since of a deep decay."

51

"This day we received an account of the death of the King of Sweden by the hands of an assassin," writes Mr. Collins a year later. "It will be of no detriment to the French Revolution as he was one of its most violent enemies. At present the trade of kings is but a very indifferent one," he adds—just how "indifferent" the world was not long in becoming aware. It was not an extra on a Philadelphia street corner, but in one of Mary's letters, many weeks old, that Tom read: "The French have at last killed their unfortunate queen. What will be the fate of the wretched children heaven only knows. I think she is happy in being relieved from a load of life; but they have sullied all their honour now, in their cowardly actions toward a poor, broken-hearted woman."

The gifted persons who, now and then, write pleasant essays, or communications to literary magazines, lamenting the decline of the letter and taking the world to task for having allowed the letter to decline seem quite unreasonably to ignore the fact that we no longer depend on this form of literature for general information.

In fact, our attitude towards general information has long since ceased to be that of dependence, for the commodity in one form or another is thrust upon us in quantities we can neither absorb nor retain. The Sunday newspaper is unwieldy with it. At countless theatres it is now reeled off at us by the thousands of yards. The library table, the table at the club, the reception room of doctor, dentist, and dressmaker, are piled high with it. At just this moment it has occurred to me to glance at the volumes on the table at which I am writing. Among the litter of current frivolities I find there that various members of the household have left two books on the American railway, *Impressions of Russia,* by George Brandes, "Tabs-Up" of the *Encyclopædia Britannica,* and three prohibitively expensive and beautifully illustrated works on the South Sea Islands, procured for nothing from the public library. We are none of us students of anything in particular, and a fortnight hence the intellectual tone and geographic scenes of this specific library table will have completely changed. It is but an ordinary instance of how nowadays the world persists in coming to one uninvited.

In 1790, however, it did not, and Mary's frequent requests for enlightenment more than anything else illustrate the difference in function between family letters of that time and today.

"I beg you may send me a detailed account of the laws, manners and customs of the inhabitants, with your thoughts on them, by the first opportunity," she writes Tom, and I realize with a smile that in none of the many, many letters I have written to relatives in foreign lands have I ever had occasion to make a similar request. The planet has shrunk incredibly in a hundred and twenty-three years, and today the world is very much with us.

"I return you many thanks for the information I have long wished for concerning the occupations of an American farmer and planter. I need no further proof of their industry and the happiness of their situation," Mary replies to what no doubt was an enthusiastic treatise by Tom on Pennsylvania agriculture. Evidently, also, he discoursed at length on the Pennsylvania

Dutch, who have since found their way into several volumes of our sectional American fiction, but his remarks, while instructive, do not seem to have been sufficiently dogmatic for his little sister. She was an extremely ethical and positive young person, and while she fancied she did not approve of hasty judgment, judgment of some kind her uncompromising young soul demanded. For in her next letter she herself rectifies her brother's omission as follows:

"In looking over the characters of the German inhabitants of your state, as you do not give your opinion or sum up their defects with their virtues, I shall attempt to give my ideas relative to them. I look on it to be the duty of every individual that either reads or writes, to turn his eyes to the bright side of any subject which presents itself to his view. We should therefore consider well before we condemn or praise any person or persons. With these thoughts in my head I took up your letter and throwing respectively the good and bad qualities of the Germans into the scale of impartiality and on taking a short time to determine, I find the former preponderate in a high degree above the latter and, as far as I can judge, there is much greater room for praise than comment.

"On the whole, I admire the Germans for their steady adherence to their own language and customs, as it argues their being possessed of that high degree of national enthusiasm which you join me in being pleased with. But they or any other as enlightened a nation are very much to blame in admitting of the veil of superstition being drawn over their eyes, which, you must confess from your own letter, they do not avoid.

"The part of Pennsylvania you are at present in must be beautifully romantic, and the next letter I receive from you I shall expect some poetic production of yours on the serenity of the country and the charms of solitude. It must be a charming country and I sincerely hope we shall one day meet and be settled on it, for I am convinced we should all be much happier on it than here, not but that my opinion is, happiness consists more in our own breasts than either in climate or country."

"I am very sorry to hear of the war you have

56

engaged in with the Indians," she declares in 1791, "as I am sure there cannot be anything so hurtful to such a rising and flourishing state as America as war, which has been the downfall of many as prosperous a settlement. But I hope it will not be her fate." Mary's concern in this racial difficulty was for the "rising and flourishing state," but it is characteristic that Tom's mother should consider it only in its possible relation to Tom. With the adorable apprehension of mothers she pictures Philadelphia overrun and looted by savage red-skinned tribes, and her relief when Tom rearranged the maternal perspective is touchingly sincere.

"The idea of your being near the place where that dreadful disorder raged made me a very wretched mother, and I thank my God that my dear Tom was so far away from it," she exclaims.

Washington and Franklin are mentioned frequently in the course of the letters, with both interest and veneration.

"I have read the speech of the great Washington at the opening of the sessions of Congress and have compared it with that of our Sovereign, but the comparison was so hurtful to the latter that I could not think of sending it to you," says Mary. "His Majesty's speech is not worth travelling so far, as it is the same that has been delivered each session of Parliament for years back. I admire General Washington's speech very much, but General Mifflin's has, I think, as much merit and I cannot suppose it so much studied."

"I request you will give me every information respecting the manner in which you were received by your friends, also an account of your situation and prospects, and give me a particular account of Dr. Franklin," writes Tom's father.

"I hope my dear brother will forgive me if I inform him that I have seen letters of his to his mother and sister, so very trifling in some parts that an impartial reader would never have judged you to be a disciple of Blackstone, or a countryman of the immortal Franklin, whose elegant simplicity of style can never be sufficiently imitated," writes John, among whose admirable qualities a sense of humour was not conspicuous.

From the first, I am sure, Mary was intensely curious about American women in general and,

in particular, the impression they produced on
her brother, but for subtle feminine reasons that
I can only suspect without attempting to divine
she does not, even to the extent of a single question, betray herself. In view of the fact that
Tom married two American women before he
was forty, his interest in them can scarcely be
doubted, and it is evident that he could not at
last endure his sister's pointed silence on so delightful a topic. As to what he wrote to Mary
one can only speculate, but here is her half-
humorous, half-sarcastic reply:

"I suppose you think it was want of taste pre-
vented my inquiring about the ladies, but you
must attribute it to my extreme ignorance,
which did not think them worth the question.
I now desire to know everything concerning
them, as from your letter, in which you speak
so highly of them, I suppose you think your
favourite beauty slighted. I beg you may tell
me her name, who she is, and as you say they are
so very agreeable, you must send me a list of
their perfections that I may regulate my conduct
accordingly; imperfections it is impossible they

should have, so I do not desire a list of them. I had even the ignorance to suppose they were all your house serfs, nor did I think they knew any of the polite wits or fashionable follies which constitute fine ladies."

Two years later Mary again administers a sweet, sisterly slap, incited without doubt by even warmer eulogies from Tom.

"I would wish (if there are any good artists in Philadelphia), when you find it perfectly convenient to your pocket, you would send me a likeness in miniature. I could get it set here. As a favourite with the ladies, I have great curiosity to see your pretty face, but you must not be angry if I say I think the American women in general are devoid of taste and, I hear, very insipid."

Tom's family worshipped him, and in their worship they were all intensely human. The young man's prosperity, his increasing number of acquaintances and friends, his brilliancy, his satisfaction—in a word, his success, gave his parents and his brother and sister genuine pleasure, but pleasure of the kind that at times is oddly indistinguishable from pain. As so often happens, they suspected that the very progress of which they were so proud led away and ever further away from themselves; and indeed, as time went on, there began to be the old, indisputable, and heart-rending evidence of it. Tom's letters, at first so frequent, regular, and comprehensive, gradually became shorter, more occasional. They did not, it seems, display the slightest decrease in affection, for the replies to them were pathetic with gratitude for the writer's protestations. But, one realizes, they were no longer the same spontaneous outlet of the boy's youthful desire for self-expression. In the law, in Philadelphia society, among all the varied interests of an ambitious young community, Tom found innumerable methods of expressing himself, and after a few years his letters to his family became but perfunctory responses in answer to a not particularly insistent call of duty.

The newspaper wit who referred to "the high cost of loving" intended, perhaps, to be no more than witty, but in his sprightly phrase there is a deep and tragic truth, even if he did not mean

61

to put it there. For, sooner or later, it always costs one something to love; and the greater the love, the higher the cost. "Aimer—c'est être utile à soi; se faire aimer—c'est être utile aux autres," is, I have grown to believe, beautifully true. But the good one does oneself by one's affection for another cannot be had for nothing or even for the affection. Its cost is high, it has to be paid for, and in a hundred different manners of human anguish—in anxiety or in grief, in disillusion or remorse, or disappointment, or bitterness, or in just unmitigable boredom sometimes—it is paid for.

The love of Mr. and Mrs. Collins for the two boys, John and Tom, was very great, and whenever I read their letters, I find myself skipping the paragraphs and hastily turning the pages in which, for their devotion to my great-grandfather, they so extravagantly paid. Even after all these years, when everybody concerned has long been dead, Tom's growing indifference, the unconscious, youthful cruelty of his neglect, still has the power to hurt and sadden. Very gentle were the first allusions to it. "I was in hopes

to have heard from you by Captain Geddes,"
Mr. Collins writes, "and I assure you I found myself very much disappointed by your silence, but
I am so well convinced of my dear boy's love and
duty that I have not an idea of its proceeding
from a want of either, and I hope in the good-
ness of Providence that indisposition has not been
the cause."

"We were at last made happy by the receipt
of your long wished for and very welcome letter
after so painful a silence as since November, it
being now almost the middle of May," records
Mary after six months had passed without news
of her brother. "You may well imagine how un-
easy we all were until the arrival of Captain
Macking, per the sloop in Sligo, which eased our
doubts concerning your happiness and welfare.

"In a state of the most distressing uncertainty
I address my dearest brother to know from what
cause or what reason we are all made wretchedly
unhappy by such unaccountable silence as his
has been now for upwards of twelve months,"
Mary writes again. But there were to be still
longer intervals; a year and a half—even two

years. It seems scarcely credible, and the pleadings of Tom's mother as she grew older, and ill with anxiety, were veritable cries of pain. I refrain from quoting them.

John was far from happy in Dublin, and he instantly wins one's interest and sympathy when it becomes clear from his own and the other letters that he was the type of boy who, in opposition to the family wishes, had set his young heart on going to sea. Extremely handsome, positive in his opinions, and restless with a physical energy that found no outlet in a series of petty clerkships, he was for some years a difficult problem. John was a very fine boy, but of the kind whose most admirable traits are not, after a certain age, developed by the restraints of domesticity. One keenly realizes that his unsatisfied desire for action and daring now and then took the form of revolts against family life, altogether disturbing to his parents and sister.

"Your brother has left Mr. White and has not gone into any other employment as yet, and indeed idleness does not go with him, for he now thinks himself so much the man that he will hear nothing from his father. As for me, his conduct is more undutiful than ever and I am sorry to say that he is not one atom steadier than when you left here. I hope in God he will see his errors before it is too late to mend them," writes Mrs. Collins.

"What your father will do with John I know not," she complains again. "It is indeed a melancholy thought to have him at his time of life not in any sort of employment whatever, but idling about this horrid place from morning till night. You know he is not a disposition for that, as an active mind must be employed, be it good or bad. He has never stuck to any sort of study one week since his return home. I wish you would ask him, as if I had not hinted to you about it, and tell him that you suppose he takes advantage of all this idle time to improve himself. Indeed your sister is a vast comfort to us."

What a comically familiar ring there is to this last! Is there anybody in the world, I wonder, who has not, with the same fatuous discretion, attempted indirectly to reach someone else in very nearly the same written words? And has the recipient of such a request ever been scrupulously true to the trust reposed in him? Tom certainly was not. Delighted, no doubt, at the chance of taking his brother to task, he wrote to John at once, and incidentally made it perfectly evident that their mother had complained of him. In John's reply there was a dignity, justice, and self-control that has always seemed to me remarkable in a thoroughly angry boy of twenty-one or two.

"You have written touching my behaviour toward my mother. I am totally unconscious of having done anything toward her which her own remonstrance would not remedy without writing to you. You tell me in your letter that the fault cannot arise from your mother. To what, then, must you attribute it? Believe me, dear Tom, for I have known it by sorrowful experience, that the fault can at times arise from the parent. However, I shall at present say no more of it, as I assure you the subject cannot be more unpleasant to you than it is to me."

I should like to dwell at length on John. From innumerable references to him in the letters his personality emerges and grows until, at the end of his brief, brave career, one shares with the family and his companions in arms the admiration and love they all came to have for him. But I may quote only two passages, one from Mary, and one from John himself.

"John, I suppose, has informed you of the great misfortune he has sustained by the removal of his friend Dominic," Mary writes. "Dominic, in my opinion, has not a grain of friendship in his composition for any person but himself, which John will not allow, though my father and mother often tell him so. Nor would he ever forgive me if he supposed that I said so or even thought so."

On realizing that the tone of one of his letters to Tom had deeply hurt his young brother's feelings, John immediately confessed the regret and remorse with which he was overcome:

"Your letter I received by the Dublin packet and I most solemnly assure you that I never yet felt more abashed at any action of mine than the writing of that ever to be execrated letter of the twelfth of August. As I am most heartily con-

67

vinced of the impropriety of my conduct I therefore request you may forgive it, attributing it to
that impetuosity of disposition to which I am at
times so subject"—a manly letter that ends with:
"Though the testimony of my love is small, I
request you to receive it as it is really intended
and believe that no alteration of time or situation
can change me from being your ever affectionate
brother and friend, John Collins." Stubbornly
loyal was John, and brave with a courage that
was moral as well as physical.

"Your brother, disliking business and wishing
to go to sea," Mr. Collins at last writes, "I got
him appointed through the very best interest in
Ireland, a midshipman on board the *Invincible,*
man-of-war of seventy-four guns, commanded
by the Hon. Capt. Thos. Packenham, and as it is
a course of life that you know he had fixed his
heart on, I did not think it prudent to prevent
his pursuing it."

From then on there was not a day of John's
young life that was not a day of pride for all of
them, and I wish it were in my power to reconstruct his gallant conduct with Lord Howe's

squadron in its long campaign against the French, of his popularity with officers and men, and of the gratifying rapidity with which he was promoted to the rank of lieutenant.

"John was in the grand engagement the first of June and received the thanks of his captain for his meritorious behaviour, and has his promise from Lord Howe of being made a lieutenant immediately," writes his father.

"I have never felt more pleasure in the idea of John's being my brother than since the first of June, that glorious epoch of English valour," declares Mary. And she goes on to describe the *Invincible's* dashing and successful activities in the engagement. And then, under Nelson, John took part in that blind, prolonged pursuit of Napoleon's fleet to Egypt, and on the 1st of August, 1798, at the Battle of the Nile—the battle that made Nelson a national hero—John was one of the two hundred and eighteen British killed.

"My dearest brother," writes Mary, "my father, mother and I wrote to you the twenty-third of last July, at which time you were informed of our father's being appointed to a lucrative situation in the island of Dominica, and that it was the intention of my mother and me to accompany him to the West Indies. I believe those letters said we expected to leave England in November or December; they also said our beloved John was a lieutenant on board the *Alexander,* then in the Mediterranean with Lord Nelson. Yes, my dearest Tom, he *was* there then, in health and spirits, esteemed and loved by all who knew him, but on the glorious 1st of August, which established England's throne and overthrew the hated and detested French and their navy; that day, replete with joy and happiness for almost every other family, tore from us the dearest, noblest, best of men—the fondest, most affectionate of sons and brothers. He fell early in the engagement, regretted by all who knew him, as he had lived beloved. He left us to mourn a loss we can never recover or forget. Would to heaven it had been my lot to have left this world could it have spared him to his father and mother, but the Almighty will must be

70

obeyed. Unable to pursue it, I must leave this subject."

In Dominica, then as now a British possession, Mr. and Mrs. Collins and Mary (the first in some official position) settled in 1799 and remained for many years. I regret that I cannot here give all their letters from the place, for they are interesting and at times dramatic. Pretty much everything that could happen on a tropical island seems to have happened, and for Tom's benefit the three record it all. The island was swept by frightful hurricanes, a neighbouring volcano (by consulting a map I suspect that it was our comparatively recent acquaintance Mount Pelee) blew up with distinct success, and Roseau, the capital of Dominica, was besieged and for a time held by the French. Of this sharp three days' fight Mr. Collins's account is graphic, and his closing paragraph is especially quaint. Having told in great detail how the French removed from Roseau to their ships everything valuable and portable upon which they could lay their hands, he adds:

"In justice to the enemy I must say the French

troops conducted themselves with the utmost propriety, but there was a rascally regiment of Italians, the very scum and outcasts of the earth, attached to them who were guilty of every enormity of which you can conceive." One is left to reflect that it is indeed a polite and charming race who can pillage a town and strip it bare "with the utmost propriety."

Mrs. Collins, my great-great-grandmother, died in Dominica, but whether her husband is with her in the Protestant cemetery at Roseau, or whether he returned to Europe with Mary, I have not been able to learn. For Mary, a widow with four daughters and almost no money (she married a young Englishman who was also in the service of the Government), set sail for Europe in 1809 with the intention of educating her little girls at Tours, in France.

How very dead they have all been until today, when—with what success I know not—I have tried for an hour or so to bring them back! How closed and over and done for! How "yellowed with age!" And yet, at times, they are all four real and near to me, for through Tom they belong to me. When, old and weary of this world, Tom's daughter (my grandmother) gladly left it, I was with her and gently closed her eyes; and when, in turn, her daughter, who was my mother, grew older and then old, the wan little hand I held in mine while she died seemed, in some sad, strange way, to be both taking from me and leaving with me everything in life that was worth while.

PEACE—PERFECT PEACE

PEACE—perfect peace! And this does not refer to the League of Nations, disarmament conferences, or the World Court. No, it is none of them I would here acclaim. Peace—perfect peace! From the depths of a happy heart the soothing words escape me, because five days ago, purely for the sake of upholding a principle, I discharged my cook. Greater courage hath no man than this. Women, so it is said, can do such things without flinching, but if beforehand I had been given a choice between this abrupt severance of diplomatic and culinary relations, and participating in a transatlantic flight, I truly believe that I should have rushed to the seaboard. Since it has happened, however, for the moment suffice it to declare that ever and anon a phrase born somewhere deep down in my immortal soul rises joyously to my lips. And the phrase is: Peace—perfect peace.

When Owen Meredith, in the second canto of *Lucille* wrote his so often quoted:

74

PEACE—PERFECT PEACE

We may live without poetry, music and art;
We may live without conscience, and live without
heart;
We may live without friends; we may live without
books;
But civilised man cannot live without cooks

when Owen Meredith wrote that, he simply did
not know what he was talking about. The real
meaning of the famous lines probably is merely
that Meredith had never tried to live without
a cook and didn't appreciate how easily it can
be done. Of course the obvious retort for him
to make to this would be that he was referring
to "civilized" people, and that I apparently could
not be included in the category. So be it. I
don't care. All I ask for the time being is to
be left alone with my new-found happiness—
the happiness of having thrown off the yoke; the
happiness of "self-determination," the "New
Freedom"—and all those things upon which the
world so incessantly brooded during a Wilsonian
age.

Often have I read and heard about the comfort to be had from a fireless cooker, but even

the comforts promised in the advertisements of them pale before the multifarious comforts of a fired cook. I had long suspected myself of being entirely competent to do everything I paid my cook to do, but until the other day the flattering suspicion had not been put to the test. Since then it has, and in doing all my own housework and cooking I find that I do it not only quite as well as did the departed one, but in certain respects much better, and in all respects I do it in about a third of the time.

Living alone, as has been my fate for the past year, a single little fairy in the home has been sufficient—indeed, more than sufficient—and she has graciously undertaken to perform certain functions in no way related to "fighting with food," as the war posters so strikingly expressed it. "General housework" is, I believe, the technical term for such activities, which include, among other things: (1) making prolonged and altogether maddening sounds with a vacuum cleaner in the room immediately above whichever room one happens to be occupying; (2) thoughtfully and conscientiously picking up every separate writing-material, letter, bill, and book on one's desk and setting it down in some other place on one's desk—a place in which it has never been before and in which it doesn't belong, and in which you can't possibly find it; and (3) day after day making one's bed in the stupid fashion in which every woman makes a bed until she is shown the right way by some man.

If there is anywhere in the world a woman who can dust a desk and, except for the dust, leave its various objects even approximately where she found them, it has never been my good fortune to make her acquaintance, and as for beds— It will be recalled that blankets are usually made in one long piece twice the length of the bed. Simply by folding it over, end to end, you have, as it were, two blankets, and the open end should always, of course, be placed at the head of the bed. By doing so the occupant of the bed can have over him one thickness of blanket or two, just as he pleases. But until a woman has been told anywhere from ten to twenty-five times, she invariably places the open end at the foot of the bed, with the result that the occupant is obliged to sleep under two thicknesses of blanket whether he wants to or not, or get up and remake his bed some time during the night. In Japan and China—in all Oriental countries, in fact—as well as in Mexico and Russia, beds are always correctly made, with the open end of the blankets at the head, because throughout the Orient, Russia, and Mexico the chambermaids are always men.

If there were anything insuperably difficult or dangerous in picking up an object from a table or a desk, flicking the dust from it, and then restoring it to its strategic base—if this occasionally necessary performance required talent, skill, strength of mind, or even unusual strength of body, I should modestly refrain from proclaiming that I can do it, because it would sound as if I were boasting. But I can do it, not only once, but over and over again—every day, in fact. My cook couldn't.

Then, too, it was interesting and highly gratifying to discover that it doesn't really take three-quarters of an hour to boil an egg, fry three thin, narrow slices of bacon, toast two pieces of bread, and make a pot of coffee. I had always assumed that it did, but, without hurrying, it takes just fourteen minutes, which includes collecting the various utensils and setting a tray. I cannot detect that I do this any better than my cook did; but I can do it quickly and without losing my temper. She couldn't.

The intense satisfaction you obtain from driving your own vacuum cleaner arises from the fact that while you are thus engaged, you cannot by any possibility be in the room underneath listening to the horrible noises it makes and wondering if it is ever going to cease.

During the first day on which I was left all alone in the world, I managed, in addition to my ordinary occupations, to achieve the following:

1. Cooked breakfast.

2. Washed the dishes and mopped the kitchen floor.

3. Fed and watered the parrot.

4. Made my bed (and made it right) and swept and dusted three rooms.

5. Kept the home fires burning.

6. Had a political discussion with the iceman.

7. Cooked luncheon.

8. Washed the dishes.

9. Discovered great lumps of damp wearing-apparel, towels, handkerchiefs, and napkins that had been washed, but not ironed, and ironed them all.

10. Ran out and voted for Al Smith.

11. Ran back again and cooked dinner.

12. Washed the dishes.

The ironing was without doubt the most fascinating thing I have done for years, and after successfully transforming 15 handkerchiefs, 11 napkins, 3 tray cloths with flounces round the edge, 13 towels, 4 suits of pyjamas, and a number of other useful articles from repellent wrinkledness to a condition of smooth and inviting beauty I came to the conclusion that the whole secret of the art of ironing consists in the way the iron sizzles after you have spit on your fingers and slapped it. You have to listen to the sizzle very attentively. If it sizzles too sharply —sort of spits back at you—it means that you are going to scorch something, but if it doesn't sizzle quite sharply enough, the iron refuses to slide smoothly back and forth; it drags and every now and then stumbles over its own feet and makes a crease. After scorching two handkerchiefs I practised for a while on a torn napkin and learned how to appraise the sizzle at its true value.

You learn very quickly to recognize the way it ought to sound to give the best results, only now and then you deceive yourself by using too much spit. The sleeves of the pyjamas were frightfully difficult, and for a while I thought I should have to give up the flounces on the tray cloths altogether. To cause them to look like flounces you have to make the iron do a kind of combined Dutch roll, outside-edge, and toe dance. However, after a while it begins to come to you, and once accomplished, a rippling, billowy flounce suddenly appears to be the loveliest phenomenon in all nature.

No, I don't need a cook. It's wonderful after all these years suddenly to discover the fact. And just because I am so well able to do without one, I have been positively besieged during the past week by a succession of determined and terrifying women who seem to have taken some sort of sacred vow that they are going to install themselves in my kitchen and do my cooking.

On every hand it has long been wailed that it is well-nigh impossible to get a cook, that cooks have disappeared from the face of the earth— that cooks have become extinct. At the sublime and awful moment of telling mine to stand not upon the order of her going I was haunted by the thought that I was doing something final— irrevocable—that it would never, never be possible to get another. But exactly three hours after her departure, during which time I had not conveyed the news of my relief and happiness to anyone, the telephone rang, and over the wire came in the most resolute tones: "I hear yeez want a cook."

She must actually have run to the telephone, because I could hear her making hoarse sounds, like a sea lion, into the receiver. Ever since then the house—by the front door, back door, telephone, and post office—has been beset; a veritable Battalion of Death. And I not only have not in

any way tried to get one; I've almost resolved
not to have one.

No cooks in the world any more? Why, the
world is swarming with cooks. The other afternoon one of them was waiting for me on the
piazza with her visiting card in her hand—a
card disclosing her to be not only a cook, but a
"caterer." Think of having your solitary meals
prepared by a caterer! You couldn't possibly
become lonely; it would make you feel like a
perpetual crowd. She came in and called on me
and all but overpowered me with her splendour.
It was just like being accorded an interview by
Madame Fremstad got up as La Tosca.

Delicately manipulating a parasol with a han-
dle about four feet long, she confided to me that
as a rule she received five dollars a day, but as so
few persons were "entertaining" just at present,
she had decided to devote all her time to vocal
music and plain cooking. I was so afraid she
might rush into the kitchen and begin to do both
at once that I told her my house was hopelessly
antique and uncomfortable, and that to live in
it necessitated hardships such as no vocalizing

83

cateress had ever been called on to endure. When she got up to go, she exclaimed, with a charming shrug and wave of the parasol: "Well, I don't think I'll try it," to which I mentally replied: "You bet you won't unless it be over my dead body."

The best way to get a cook, apparently, is not to want one. Once you have made up your mind that you don't need one, they come and beg you to eat from their hand.

ARRIVAL

[1]

WITHOUT doubt the ideal fashion in which to approach the Balearic Islands would be that adopted by Saint Raimundo de Penyafort in 1232 for departing from them. To some travellers this procedure at the outset might present certain difficulties, as it necessitates being a saint in good standing, but it would be the most agreeable as well as the most inexpensive way of making the journey. King Jaime I, the splendid young monarch—"El Conquistador"—who in 1229 had conquered the Moors and driven most of them from Majorca, was making a third expedition to the island for the purpose of negotiating with several thousand of the vanquished race who proudly refused to surrender to anyone but the king in person. Jaime was only between nineteen and twenty at the time, and, as has always been known, kings will be boys. According to one of the chronicles, Jaime, to the annoyance and scandal of Saint Raimundo, was in the habit of mitigating the tedium of statecraft more often with the presumably charming co-operation of one Doña Berenguela de Fernandez than with high thinking and prayer; and the saint, as saints will, expostulated with him. The young sovereign, however (throughout a reign of sixty years he was every inch a king), did not hesitate to tell the godly man where, as it were (or, rather, as it would be today), "to get off at," and the situation became decidedly strained; so strained, in fact, that the saint announced his intention of leaving for Barcelona unless Jaime straightway began to see life steadily and see it whole. The young monarch could not quite bring himself in so many words to forbid a saint's departure, but he sought to achieve the same end by issuing a decree prohibiting vessels bound for the mainland from transporting ec-clesiastics. This naturally should have closed the incident, but as Raimundo, after all, was a most holy man, it just supernaturally did not. From the dock at the little port of Soller, he spread his cloak on the water, fearlessly em-barked upon it, and in due time sailed into Barcelona—a trifle of a hundred and forty-three miles away—where the whole town had gathered along the shore to acclaim his arrival. To this spirited, not to say spiritual, aquatic event there were eyewitnesses innumerable, and, besides, at the port of Soller the exact stone from which Saint Raimundo stepped to his hastily improvised but adequate craft can be seen at any time.

Yes, undoubtedly the perfect approach to the Balearic Islands would be all alone at the prow of one's motor-coat, preferably, perhaps, of one's mackintosh—as, for some not wholly explicable reason, every foreign visitor even to Palma, the largest city and the capital of the most important of the five islands, appears to enjoy the delusion that about his journey there is something explorative, romantic, almost daring. In fact, one of the locality's innumerable engaging attributes is its perennial ability to stir in the least imaginative of tourists emotions akin to those of a Columbus, a Marco Polo, a Magellan, a Peary, or a Scott; and persons who write about the Balearics are given to defining their impressions with titles like "The Forgotten Isles," "The Lost Isles," "The Enchanted Isles." Yet, since the time of the Carthaginians, the Ligurians (whoever they were), the Phœnicians, the Greeks, Romans, Vandals (the Goths, for some reason, did not bother about the islands), Moors, Spaniards, French, as well as those territorial connoisseurs the British, the islands of Majorca, Minorca, Iviza, Cabrera, and Fomentera, while often enough they have been stolen, have never been strayed, lost, or forgotten, and upon lands however beautiful that continue to produce a population so sturdy, active, and industrious, so admirably sensible and competent, enchanting rather than enchanted would be a more accurate term to bestow.

Of late years that once gratifying old phrase "off the beaten track" has acquired a new significance, for no place to which any normal human being has the slightest desire to go is nowadays off the beaten track. At the time of writing, the summit of Mount Everest is said to be somewhat arduous of access, but it probably will not long remain so and anyhow the normality of persons who wish to visit it is at least open to debate. Rather than suggestive of a locality, the words have come to be illuminative of the point of view of those who employ them. A prominent citizen of Omaha recently confided in me that for him, one of Majorca's chief charms was in its being "off the beaten track," but I feel quite sure that the equally prominent citizens of Palma who from time to time ship their touring cars to Barcelona, and from there motor in a few days to San Sebastian, Biarritz, Deauville, and Paris might be able, for precisely the same reason, to discover a hitherto shrouded charm in Omaha. For more thousands of years than historians can bring themselves to agree on, the Balearics in general and Majorca in particular have been decidedly in the track rather than off it, and today Palma often recalls the words of an aged Bostonian who used to be fond of telling me that his country place at Nahant was "aloof rather than apart."

The aloofness of Majorca constitutes a kind of backhanded tribute to those invaluable compilations, Baedeker's guide to Spain, and the *Encyclopædia Britannica*. If either had been more humanly expansive on the subject—less suc-

cinctly accurate—the island long since might
have become a bigger, better, and more boresome
Mont Saint-Michel, for in most discussions as
to its exact locality (and none of one's travelled
acquaintances who have not been there ever
knows just where it is or to whom it belongs)
the encyclopædia is finally resorted to. Longi-
tude, latitude, and ownership having been determined, the topic would at once languish and
expire, if the one unappeasable party to every
geographical dispute did not then produce a
small, sweat-stained, crimson volume from the
short row of other and identical small, sweat-
stained, crimson volumes without which no cultured American family can afford to be and
proceed to read the bald if lucid postscript of
the methodical Hun. The encyclopædia and
Baedeker have not done right by our Nell, and
it is doubtful if anyone's impetus to visit the
Balearics ever came from them.

My own certainly did not, and until a few
years ago, when, at the devitalizing hour of six
A.M., I disembarked and at last found myself
on the long, impressively solid dock and break-

water of Palma, my information on the subject was scarcely more definite than that of a widely travelled compatriot to whom I sat next at dinner some months later in Paris. When in answer to her conversational hors d'œuvres I replied that I had spent the winter on the island of Majorca, she looked prettily vague for an instant and then, a great light dawning, confidently exclaimed: "Oh yes, of course—nowadays everyone goes to the South Seas." It is not literature or even reading-matter that seems to send one to Majorca, for although, later on, one discovers that much has been written about it—all of it informative and some of it agreeable—the volumes in question have never achieved popularity or, even among the globe-trotters, a wide circulation. Not long ago none of the solemnly erudite, low-voiced, expensively miseducated clerks in four of New York's largest bookshops had ever heard of the Balearic Islands, and from their illimitable seas of "travel books" we succeeded in dredging not a paragraph. Nevertheless, a whole libraryful has been written about them, and with the exception of the late Austrian Archduke Luis Salvator's exhaustive work called *Die Balearen im Wort und Bild*—the kind of obese, monumental opus drolly known in Germany as a "Handbuch"—I once, with a view to finding out what to avoid, read nearly all of it. Many of the volumes have been written by cultivated British ladies, and all over the world the travels of British ladies appear to be in the nature of prolonged, joyous, botanical frenzies, the recorded impressions of the countries they have visited being given to tense, colourful passages that read something like this:

For an hour or more the dear little fields were veritable carpets of the scarlet ranunculus, the Adonis vernalis, and the handsome crimson and yellow scrophularia, while further along the blue borage, pink allium, convolvulus, gorse, and mallow were rather more in evidence. The heights were quite feathery with the pinus maritima— and oh, the scent of the wet cistus bushes!

However, with a little practice in reading the sometimes delightful opera of British ladies who have spent the winter in Palma, one learns to feel this sort of seizure coming on and rapidly turns a page or two until, in the words of the infant Macaulay when a maladroit visitor spilled a cup of hot coffee on his little legs, "Madam, the agony is abated."

Most reasons for spending a week, a month, a year, or, as now and then happens, the rest of one's life on the island are likely to be good ones, although my own reason, I confess, sounds singularly idiotic. For it consists solely in the fact that at least forty years ago I heard a verse beginning: "There was an old man of Majorca" and immediately decided that some day I should go there. I had not the slightest idea of where Majorca was or to whom it belonged and it was only after several decades that I inquired; but even then no one could tell me the customary method of approach and I have never come across anybody who could quote the verse, which, except for the first line, I had long since forgotten. However, old men whose activities are exploited according to this particular metrical formula are never, it seems, very nice old men—never refined, Christian gentlemen exactly, whether they hail from Siberia, Algeria, or Siam; so no doubt it is just as well that I am unable to recall this one's claim to immortal infamy. He did, though, send me to Majorca, and for that one should be, if one could, lyrically grateful.

Palma can be reached with equal facility from Hither or Yon, and while, often since, I have arrived from Hither, my first approach was distinctly from Yon; from, in fact, North Africa. For some reason only possible to conjecture, tourist agencies until recently have had a mysterious gloom on the Balearic Islands. One of the last few localities of the world left for them to exploit and ruin, they have never done so, possibly because of difficulties with the often autocratic Spanish steamship companies, perhaps because of a reluctance on the part of Palma's leading citizens to concede anything definite or sufficiently lucrative in the matter of projected hotels. But, whatever the underlying cause, the employees of tourist agencies, at best, managed to convey to one the impression that they knew nothing about the islands and, at worst, that, knowing all about them, they did not consider

them worth a visit. At Algiers, for instance,
Thomas Cook and his sons were even more positively discouraging. Authoritatively they at
first declared that there was no direct communication between Algiers and Palma, but when
confronted with the irrefutable fact that there
monthly was, they conveyed, with the professional civility which on occasion can achieve
such sublime heights of insolence, that, of course,
if I were the sort of person who enjoyed fourteen hours of filth, cockroaches, uneatable food,
and objectionable associates, it was no affair of
theirs. But once on board the little ship that
every month leaves the mainland of Spain and
makes a round trip, stopping at various diverting
places—Oran, Algiers, Palma, Marseilles among
them—it was a question whether this was sheer
ignorance or deliberate malice. For the tiny
steamer, while far from luxurious, was immaculate (contrary to the popular Anglo-Saxon belief, most Spanish houses, hotels, and ships are
immaculate) and, in the somewhat austere
Iberian fashion, which one learns to respect, comfortable. From any of half a dozen low-hung

wicker chairs on the upper deck one could watch the gradual, late-afternoon fade-out of Algiers and speculate on why a city so ethereal—so dreamlike—from the sea, should on closer inspection prove so tawdry, so trashy, so squalid. The captain's courteous although not demonstrative black setter (long since, he had become blasé in the matter of lodgers for the night) was a sympathetically domestic note, and it soon became evident that except for half a dozen men hidden away somewhere in the second class or steerage, and seventy-five or a hundred sheep piteously and vacuously bleating in the hold, Clark and I were the only passengers. Four amiably conversational stewards attended to our wants at a dinner that proved endurable to any one whose endurance is adequate to Spanish dinners (mine is, sometimes, for a week or ten days), and all but tucked us up when we went to bed. Spanish servants, however, are a chapter in themselves.

If Yon is North Africa, Hither is of course the Spanish mainland, and from Barcelona there are several even more agreeable steamers—like large yachts they are—leaving for Palma four times a week. Until one comes to understand it, there is all the year round on these ships a surprising amount of traffic, but even a short acquaintance with the island makes it clear. Palma is a city of some sixty-five or seventy thousand inhabitants, and while in my complete ignorance of it I did not suspect it of being a prosperous, wealthy, even bustling centre of industry and trade, it actually is. The steamers carry to and fro a never-ending invasion of buyers and sellers—business men of every kind—and, in addition to these, extremely numerous families are perpetually crossing to visit relatives and, the visit terminated, crossing back again. There are still on the island magnificent estates owned by the nobility, as well as hundreds of less pretentious country places and seaside residences, as in summer Majorca for centuries has been popular with Spaniards of the mainland cities who enjoy for a few months leading a more or less patriarchal existence far from the great world. Then, too, Palma is an important garrison town. The place swarms with officers and soldiers—cavalry, artillery, infantry—who are constantly being sent over or returned. Not many of the ships arrive or depart without large theatrical companies; Palma is devoted to dramatic art in whatever guise it chooses to display itself. Of late years, also, the tourist has been more frequently appearing—British for the most part, but with an ever-increasing representation of Americans and a sprinkling of Germans and French. Altogether it is advisable to take one's passage either coming or going, in the morning as soon as possible after the ticket office has opened its doors, as, for some undivulged reason, the steamship company does not permit one to make reservations and buy tickets except on the day of sailing.

[2]

It is a mistake to approach Majorca by way of Africa. After that uninterrupted debauch of colour and squalor, that chaos of races—pure white, impure white, basalt-black, black, chocolate éclair, café au lait, buff, and baked potato—

98

the desert, the palm groves, the camels—the semi-fusion of both the worst and the best of barbarity with both the best and the worst of French colonialism—after, in short, Algiers, Constantine, Tunis, Biskra (for all time vulgarized· beyond redemption by Mr. Robert Hichens), Palma, especially at half past six on a bleak February morning, in a high wind with splashes of cold rain, at first appears to be disappointingly normal, prosaic, even markedly drab. It is impossible now to recall just what I expected, for no doubt one always does expect something, even if the anticipatory vision hovers and dissolves somewhere just beyond the vividly conscious; but, whatever it was, Palma did not in the least resemble it. In no wise, naturally, was this the fault of Palma.

To one who has never been—as the French with pleasing exactitude express it—"matinal," the fact that one invariably comes in sight of the island at dawn and steams into Palma's ravishing bay at about six A.M. is a recurrent little personal tragedy. For the bay of Palma *is* ravishing. In comparison, declares Havelock Ellis, "Naples is

but a vast, miscellaneous, water-washed boulevard." But I am not "matinal" and never have
been. I was never one of those fabulous children
whose "tired eyelids" close on "tired eyes" "the
moment the head touches the pillow." Ever
since I can remember anything, I have resented
having to go to bed and loathed having to get
up, and even now I can suffer an almost physical
anguish if I recall the years at school when every
morning at 8:45 I was compelled with the others
to greet the new day in a sullen, discordant, joyous burst of song as follows:

Hail, smiling morn, smy-il-ing morn, smy-il-ing
    morn,
Whose rosy fingers ope-enn, whose rosy fingers
    ope-enn,
Whose rosy fingers ope the gay-ates of day,
Ope the gay-ates of day,
Whose rosy fingers ope the gates of day.

To persons so, no doubt unfortunately, con-
stituted, the various exquisite phenomena of the
early hours are something as a rule perfectly
evident, but rarely felt. I have assisted at the

100

accouchement of many mornings, but my reaction to their incontestable loveliness has almost always been like one's unimpaired awareness of weather conditions while standing beside the open grave of somebody for whom one cared. Early on a fair morning at any season the approach to Palma is an experience of all but matchless beauty, and oh, how I hate it!

Still, even I could not be oblivious of the splendid solidity of Palma's long breakwater (the Muele, or, as the British call it, the Mole) with its commodious docks and commanding promenade, which thrusts far into the harbour and ends in a lighthouse—chunky, even squat, but, like all lighthouses, incorruptibly chaste (only in lighthouses has architecture succeeded in expressing impregnable chastity) and the overpowering fashion in which the Cathedral, on a slight elevation almost at the water's edge, dominates the compact, high-keyed little city behind and on two sides of it. The situation of most Spanish cathedrals indeed, of most cathedrals everywhere has, with the passage of time and the

101

growth of municipalities, become unfortunate. Toledo's colossal morgue can, from the outside, scarcely be seen at all; those of Seville and Barcelona are nearly as obscured. The great edifice at Palma, however, astonishingly appears to sail the sea like a gigantic stone and many-buttressed Noah's ark, or rears from the harbour like a more intellectually conceived and executed Rock of Gibraltar.

Alongside the ship the scene on the dock, one notes with an indefinite sense of frustration, might be that of pretty much any small European port on a wan, grey, early morning: a straggling row of conventionally clad male relatives and friends expectantly peering upward at the passengers leaning on the ship's rail—sudden ascertainments, quick, expressive facial transitions, hat-removals, hand-wavings, affectionate jocosities. Just behind them is a shelter from the rain—a corrugated roof on iron supports, and on the other side of that a short line of motor cars—two large, well-cared-for, coruscating hotel autobusses, three or four taxicabs unequipped with taximeters (it is an honest, un-

contaminated race, the Majorcan)—some Fords
in exile. But at the further end of these convenient banalities the appraising eye pauses in
both amusement and delight, for there are horses,
ten or a dozen of them, and not horses only, but
plump, sleek, strong, proud horses, attached
singly or in pairs to lightly fanciful, distinctly
humorous, sometimes two-, sometimes four-
wheeled, brownish yellow, white canvas-topped
vehicles of a model one has never before seen
anywhere. (One later learns that except on the
Balearic Islands they do not exist.) Their con-
cave, wooden bodies, ornamented with a series
of neat moulding, applied vertically, are high
off the ground; their entrances, approached by
two narrow steps are in the rear; their canvas
tops are as undefiled as if freshly laundered; and,
while you realize that these blithe chariots are
designed for the conveyance of human beings,
they have a gay, whimsical, general air of having
been dedicated solely to the transportation of
cream puffs, macaroons, lady fingers, and all
such less indelicate members of the pastry family.
One immediately plans to inquire about these

large, horse-drawn toys, to take a drive in one,
perhaps even to own one.

Since the great war for peace on earth and
the brotherhood of man my passport, signed by
Charles E. Hughes, had been skewered day and
night almost to my quivering flesh with a stout,
brass didy-pin and was at any hour instantly
produceable. On arriving from Hither, it of
course is not demanded. Yon, however, being
a French possession, travellers from its shores,
with the international urbanity that then (and
even now) everywhere obtained, are naturally
suspect of something, although it is doubtful if
anyone knows just what. A bored officer, in-
haling a cigarette between yawns, is present in
the ship's dining-room at the inspection, chiefly,
it would seem, for the purpose of ignoring it, as
the actual labour is performed by a capable
young civilian clerk armed with a fountain-pen
and a rubber stamp. Evidently his official routine
has in no wise vitiated his sense of humour, as,
after a keen, explorative glance at me, he breaks
into a boyish smile on examining my affixed
photograph, which is obviously a striking por-

trait of the kind of Baptist or Methodist minister who elopes with the pretty little eighteen-year-old choir soprano and, before being taken in adultery, manages to put in three weeks of agreeable sin at Asbury Park or Atlantic City. But while the photograph furnishes more than sufficient evidence for the justifiable arrest and detention of its original on any charge whatever, I am passed as at least technically impeccable, and permitted to land.

Then, for my luggage, on board again and into the dark hold with a cargador, the sheep with which the hold was jammed now pressing against our legs, now shrinking from us, and ceaselessly bleating on every note of two octaves. The lugubriously polite little head porter of the Gran Hotel, in the livery of his predecessor, who, I deduce, had been seven feet tall and fat, leads us to one of the smart autobusses, which, while I am sleepily wondering why hotel porters are so rarely natives of the country to which they are accredited (exotically this one turns out to be a Czecho-Slovak—or perhaps he was even a Lett), begins in the hypercivilized fashion of voluptuously padded hotel autobusses to glide along the not too well-paved causeway towards the town.

On the way there is a brief stop at the custom house, where its three uniformed and heavily armed officials are more evidently bored by their life-work than was the passport official who did not examine my passport. The two small but heavy trunks, the two large, yellow leather bags, the bundle of coats and rugs, and the revolting wicker suit-case I always at the last moment repugnantly manage to acquire, are laboriously removed from above and strung along the low, wooden operating-table; one of the trunks is even unstrapped and unlocked. But this, it seems, is going a trifle too far, for with an alarmed expression as of: "The next thing and you'll have the lid wide open," the chief inspector makes a just perceptible authoritative gesture of his brown and distinguished right hand—such as Charles V might have made in terminating a tedious audience—and all my belongings are once more hoisted to the roof.

Palma is not a city of distances, magnificent

106

or otherwise, and the swift drive from the dock to the hotel—half a mile at the most—is so brief and so saturated with interest that on unexpectedly arriving I feel defrauded by not having walked. A long row of rugged, rough-used sailing vessels, weather-stained and weather-beaten, moored side against side to the dock—*Santa María, Santa Ana, Alfredo, Palomita, Aguila,* one half guesses, half makes out; freight boats probably that circumnavigate the island and perhaps venture now and then as far as Minorca and Iviza. Slow, cumbersome, but invincibly resolute and staunch they look. One's sudden, instinctive belief and trust in them is somehow reinforced by the little family groups—a man, a woman, some children, a baby, a bare-legged sailor or two, a dog, and a cat gathered in sheltered corners of the decks around the morning coffee-pot. Across a broad avenue extending along the water front, where the harbour bristles with the perky masts of tiny pleasure craft gently rocking at anchor, and before one passes beyond, a glimpse of arcaded façades—a bicycle repair shop in the fragment of what was once an

architecturally proud church—a noble-looking,
square, stone, Gothic something (but what?)
with castellated corners and surmounted by an
open balustrade through whose pattern gleams
the sky. A double row of half-grown palm-trees,
the laudable if belated civic endeavour to live
up to one's historic name—and next, an ample,
gently inclined boulevard with a spacious, stone-
paved, tree-bordered centre for pedestrians and
a narrow roadway on either side. At this season
the trees are leafless, but their size, their age, their
central situation, and the massive stone benches
under them proclaim their importance in the
community's summer life. Heavily uddered,
modern-faced, simpering, wholly unsuccessful,
reclining stone sphinxes, not unlike the sphinxes
near the Pont Royal, a stone bandstand, simple,
graceful, really elegant—a circular basin of intensely blue and white tiles—more arcaded façades—a gushing fountain presided over by a
stone obelisk resting on four bronze turtles—an
ancient-Greek-looking girl who pauses in the filling of her ancient-Greek-looking pottery jar to
watch us turn the corner. Then all at once a

108

high, incredibly ornate and lamentable edifice—
the falsest of notes (modern Spain is a prolonged
carillon of them)—deliberately, wilfully hideous
both outside and in—the Gran Hotel.

To a Spanish hotel "matinal" has no more
applicability than it has to me, and at seven in
the morning the Gran Hotel of Palma is not at
its best. In Spain you are everywhere expected
to break your fast in your bedroom, and if an
early arrival renders this admirable custom
pointless and you decide to have your coffee or
chocolate downstairs, you soon become aware of
being regarded as an insufferable nuisance. Two
or three moody and dishevelled servants, not as
yet presentable to the public eye, will be
languidly eliminating the disorder of the night
before. The corners of rugs will be rolled back;
mournful clusters of coffee cups and sticky-
looking liqueur-glasses mutely plead to be removed and bathed; uncountable half-smoked
cigarettes and burnt matches beg to be swept up
—put out of their misery—while the only function of the furniture appears to be that of patiently sustaining other furniture upside down.

At any other hour Spanish servants are an engaging, a really adorable class, but during the first daily chapter of Genesis they sulk about their tasks, quite unmistakably regretting that you didn't die somewhere on the way; and when, at the Gran Hotel, you at last seek the detestable and terrifying little electric "lift" for the purpose of ascending to your room on the fifth floor, you are nearly always confronted by the printed sign: "No functiona." The lift but rarely "functionas," and when it does, you wish it hadn't. Its floor space is not much more than that of an ordinary barrel, and it is supposed to respond to the pressure of a bewildering row of black buttons. Stuck on occasions innumerable somewhere between the cellar and the roof, I have perforce made the acquaintance of literally everyone sojourning for the time on the premises. Immured together in a flour-barrel, one is now and then almost humanely spoken to even by the aunt of a British bishop. I do not unduly stress this odious contrivance. At first no more than an avoidable annoyance, it in the end hangs in mid-air symptomatically, symbolically. It sheds

light on Spanish temperament and character.
The servants intermittently tinker with the lift,
discuss it, make reports on it, hang the "No Functiona" sign on it, and then, for days at a time,
forget about it. It is significant that the sign
is a permanent item of the hotel's equipment,
held the year round in readiness. The year
drifts by—a new one begins—old ladies helpless
with rheumatism, and retired generals in the last
stages of asthma, seek their respective chambers,
but the lift "no functionas."

[3]

Fortuitously my room at the Gran Hotel was
the top-floor, corner room, with a circular balcony of carved stone (it was the only one vacant), and while it is the barest, most ascetic of
cubicles, it is, for a short stay at least, greatly to
be recommended. Except for the spires, the
towers, and the belfries of churches and convents, it is higher than most of the buildings
adjacent, and at every hour of the day it commands that which one hesitates to slight with a

111

word less magniloquent than "panorama." It
is the kind of panorama, too, of which one does
not tire; just the play of light and shade in these
islands is an hourly drama, even if from the fifth-
floor balcony the immediate foreground were
not usually replete with intimate and revealing
detail. And from no other point of vantage
(at least from none available to a traveller) does
one get just the same impression of two characteristic features of the town's daily life: the flat
roofs and the dovecotes. Most of Palma's
streets are so narrow—such dim serpentine passages between stone houses four or five stories
high that from this elevation all but one of them
—the broad thoroughfare along which one came
from the dock—are invisible. As seen from
above, the place is compact of masonry and
stucco except where, here and there, a green bil-
low tumbles over a pink or white or buff wall,
or the fronds of a palm have at last patiently
escaped into light and air from some damp courtyard; and one feels that by scaling the low bar-
ricades, picking one's way among the jars of
roses and geraniums, the chromatic family wash,

112

the chickens, the turkeys, the dogs, and the cats
that decorate and inhabit the city's housetops,
it would be possible to wander on the roofs from
end to end of the place and at its farther edge
finally emerge among the bare, indented, at
times snow-capped mountains. They are twenty
or more miles distant, these mountains, and at
their highest they reach an altitude of only 4,700
feet, but, with the duplicity of all properly constructed mountain ranges, they manage to appear as if they were both Alps and "just across
the way." Nearer still, on the right of the harbour, which from the balcony one does not see,
rises a densely wooded hill of vast extent and
placid, soothing regularity of outline that cul-
minates in the perfectly preserved castle of
Belver—a late thirteenth-century castle, the
castle of a historical novel in certain lights, and
in others the castle of a fairy-tale; a Hans Christian Andersen, Brothers Grimm, and Maxfield
Parrish castle; in short, the most castly of castles.

Although even in Spain on hearing that a community of but sixty-odd thousand has forty-
eight or fifty churches you at first suspect that

someone has been boasting, a brief reconnaissance from the balcony during breakfast inclines you to believe that the estimate is conservative. Without field glasses I counted twenty-three institutions of unmistakably religious import, and with them three others easily presented themselves; this, although only part of the town, is spread out below. The Cathedral, infinitely more Gothic and spiritual than when seen from the water, is just opposite and, as usual, higher, more massive, more completely in control of the general situation than anything else; while the heavy old hexagonal tower of the Church of San Nicolás, moss-grown and sprouting weeds from neglected crevices, lifts itself, tired but bravely, from a near-by irregular-shaped public plaza that contains trees, shrubs, flowers, a cabstand, the magnificently non-committal façade of the Palacio Sforteza, and a circular tin urinal of convenient if somewhat excessive visibility. As far as the city extends, there are, at intervals, an incredible number of architectural reminders that, until saved, the soul is a serious liability; aged, unpretentious belfries, most of them, of

114

buff stone, gently, even tenderly weathered to the warm, soft tint locally referred to as "tostado." It has the tone of the precipitous cliffs that skirt the harbour to the right, the tone of all the ancient buildings as well as many of the new ones, the tone of the Majorcan skin—the tone of race and the tone of time. More than any other building material it seems, throughout the centuries, to have absorbed and retained the benigner humours of an often merciless sun. Substantial, unadorned, now flat-topped, now with a sloping, pointed roof of tiles, sometimes no more than a curved or pointed arch above a suspended bell, the satisfying beauty of these small campaniles is in their proportions, their simplicity, their age, their quiet symbolization of an unquestioning faith.

For the traveller from Morocco there is in Palma's housetops existence no novelty, but one is surprised to find it, after so many generations, still being lived in Spain. Most of the inhabitants would be incredulous, shocked perhaps, to hear that in utilizing their small tiled roofs to the extent to which they do, they are only ex-

115

emplifying an instinct, antique, subconscious, and indisputably Moorish.

The men of the family spending the greater part of the day in their shops and offices, their clubs or favourite cafés, the roofs are frequented chiefly by the women and children—in itself an Oriental touch reminiscent of the zenana, although of course Majorcan women are not in any way sequestered. In this compactly built town the roof is a convenient spot on which to wash and dry clothes as well as one's long, black hair; much mending, dressmaking, embroidery, and conversation take place on the roof, and the live-stock reared there—chickens, turkeys, and babies as a rule, although I have seen ducks and an occasional lamb—require constant attention. There are always flowers to be watered and tiles to be scrubbed, for the Majorcans are ardent, even passionate scrubbers who take an almost Dutch delight in pails, brooms, mops, and the reckless swashing of soapsuds. Near by, eight or ten champion heavyweight nuns in habits of robin's-egg blue and long, white veils ascend to their roof for exercise when not engaged with

116

their classes and devotions. With hands folded
across their grandiose bosoms, they promenade
back and forth like passengers on the deck of a
ship—a consecrated barge, heaven-bound. And
they object, these majestic virgins of sixty-odd,
to being peered at and admired—at least by a
gentleman with field glasses on a balcony half a
block away. Catching me at it one morning,
they broke ranks in confusion and hastily shrank
backwards out of sight down a kind of skylight.

The inescapable drawback to the Gran Hotel's
top-floor rooms is that neither Palma's church-
bells nor its poultry has as yet accepted the re-
strictions of the eight-, or even the ten-, twelve-,
or twenty-four-hour day. Throughout the
night the bells at intervals abruptly break into
startling clangors, or gravely and interminably
toll for someone whose immortal soul has just
made the first hop-off on its way to purgatory,
and the Majorcan chanticleer is cursed either
with insomnia or with more than his customary
delusion that he controls the sun's rising. He
begins to issue shrill, impatient mandates at ten
P.M. sharp, and throughout the entire night

never for more than two or three minutes at a time abandons hope. With only eight or a dozen feet of intervening space it is practically like trying to sleep in a chicken coop, which in rural Mexico I have more than once been obliged to do.

At first the oddly shaped, various-sized, flimsy-looking, open-worked, wooden structures that, all over the town, have been added to so many of the roofs are a mystery, as, during the day, they are deserted. But just at sunset these "bare, ruined choirs" become the stages for one of the prettiest of ceremonies—the homecoming of the pigeons. Where and how these great flocks spend the day I have never learned; one sees but few pigeons in the squares and streets of the town. Yet in the late afternoon they hasten back by the thousands—wheeling, dipping, rising, circling round and round the wooden cotes for half an hour sometimes before they can be induced to make a landing and retire for the night; for apparently they have to be induced. Every flock knows its own domicile and, from afar, sails to it without hesitation or deviation, but, once arrived, it appears unable to make up its collective mind, although in one respect the functioning of this collective mind is as exquisite and as inexplicable as anything in nature. Three flocks, for instance, of say thirty, fifty-five, and sixty-two birds respectively will occupy cotes on adjoining roofs. Time and again while, with amazing swiftness, they wheel and dip round and round them, they cross one another's orbits and for an instant become one flock of a hundred and forty-seven pigeons instead of three flocks of thirty, fifty-five, and sixty-two; but for an instant only. Even before one has time in which to speculate on how they can ever extricate themselves—contrive to maintain their group integrity—they are once more three units of exactly the same numbers as before. In spite of the close formation and extreme rapidity, there have been no collisions, no sundering of family ties. Among wild geese and wild ducks one suspects a master intellect at the apex of the arrowhead, but pigeons swoop in clouds rather than in precise, geometrical alignment; some sort of consummate "uniformity in multiplicity" rather than

119

leadership would seem to be their secret. Many years ago, while sitting in a philosophy course at the erudite and charming feet of George Santayana, I heard much of "uniformity in multiplicity" but it was not until evening after evening I watched the returning pigeons of Palma that I began to have a glimmer of what the phrase perhaps meant. Presumably the pigeons wish to be at home or they would not go there; but it is evident that, once arrived, every flock is unanimous in its determination not to go to bed. Like mercurial children confronted by a similar doom, they have to be persuaded and cajoled, the persuader and cajoler being a boy or a man who stands on each roof slowly waving a long, thin wand to the end of which is attached a narrow strip of cloth and from time to time blowing a sweet lugubrious note on a whistle. By both pole and whistle the whirling groups are hypnotized, but not quite. For twenty minutes or more as they wheel and soar upward towards the western light, their pearl bellies and white underwings continue to flash like silver until at last someone succumbs to the lure, precariously flutters for a moment on one of the wooden supports or on the cajoler's head or shoulder, and succeeds in breaking the charm. The example is infectious; others at once begin to follow it, and soon a whole numerous family has surrendered for the night. Just why there is about this little performance always something affecting—poignant—it would be difficult to say. The sunset hour—the homing instinct—the rhythm of flight—the slender, muezzin-like silhouettes of the men and boys on the roofs—the long soft wail of the whistles. No doubt it is all strictly practical and needful, but it is touched too with an endearing pathos. You go indoors feeling that you are perhaps destined to care for this island.

THE COLONEL'S HAT

For many years in our front hall the head of a noble elk has served in the submissive capacity of a hatrack, and during that time its twelve formidable prongs have been the temporary resting place of a large, and now and then an interesting, number of hats. French, Italian, British, German, Spanish hats have, of course, hung there in profusion. But there have likewise been Japanese and Chinese hats, and the hats of Russia and Mexico. We used to have a good many visitors in the course of a year, and in the course of nearly fifty years the recollection of their numbers becomes impressive.

And with the exception of one, who wore a turban and did not remove it, they all wore hats. As I never make use of the elk myself, there is at the present moment, however, but a single hat upon it, and I have just taken it down for the first time in years and carefully examined it with genuine emotions that are mingled with reverence, affection, and pride.

THE COLONEL'S HAT

This one is not only an American hat; it seems to me to be, in many ways, quite the most comprehensively and distinctly American hat I have ever been privileged to hold in my hands. For one afternoon in North Dakota thirty-two years ago Theodore Roosevelt removed it from his own head and placed it on mine and then characteristically roared and shook with mirth at my complete extinguishment.

It is an enormous "cowpuncher" of the heaviest grey felt, but instead of having a stiff, flat brim like most of those made today, the brim has a slight upward turn and is bound in grey silk. When he wore it, it was adorned with a narrow band of embossed leather, and as he removed this, and undoubtedly detected the disappointment in my avaricious, fifteen-year-old eyes, he hastened to say: "I wish I could give you this, too, but it was a present from one of the cowboys at the ranch."

Examining this souvenir of Colonel Roosevelt's Western life, a few moments ago, with a minuteness I have never before bestowed upon it, has revealed what, on looking back now, seems

123

the quaintest of prophecies. For still faintly visible in the centre of the faded blue satin lining is the maker's trade-mark stamped in gilt, and it consists of an American shield upheld on one side by an eagle, and on the other by some wild animal, the exact nature of which the passage of time has rendered uncertain. Furthermore, the patent-leather sweatband has a name which, by blowing away the obliterating dust, I discovered to be, of all the words in the English language, the most significant and the most appropriate to ornament the sweatband of a hat destined, until almost the end, to be thrown into "the ring." The name the singularly clairvoyant, if all-unconscious, inventor had bestowed upon his leather band was "The Fray."

On looking back, too, there is romance and drama in the fashion in which, as it hung year after year in our front hall, the hat gradually acquired an increasing interest and importance. Such interest as it first had began and ended with me alone and springs solely from the facts that I was fifteen years old and the hat was the kind worn by cowboys. It took up a good deal of

room on the elk's head, and more than this there
was nothing to say about it. All families have
their own amiable if not especially brilliant jokes,
and it was one of ours now and then, when leaving the house with strangers, to put on the enormous affair, as if with the intention of wearing
it down town. But when asked, as on such hi-
larious occasions we invariably were, where on
earth it had come from, there was at that period
nothing whatever to reply beyond the fact that
it had been given to me "by a man in Dakota."
The very first prestige it acquired in my eyes
from having belonged to any particular man was
the prestige of its having been worn by someone
who had written a book.

At my sister's tiny cottage, on a hill in the outskirts of Mandan, Mr. Roosevelt, aged twenty-
eight, had spent part of every day walking, for
what sounded like miles, back and forth in his
room, stopping from time to time to put down
a sentence in the small, cramped unformed hand
of a careful schoolboy; and with a mixture of
awe at being in the presence of literary genesis,
and amusement that anyone so grown up could

125

still possess such a handwriting, I had, while he was out, examined one of the pages of his manuscript.

When the book was published and I had actually seen and read parts of it, the hat all at once assumed a significance and a value with which cowboys had nothing to do. It was no longer merely a cowboy hat, it was the hat of an author; moreover, the only author of my acquaintance. Since then its many metamorphoses have been, in the whole annals of hats, among the most surprising and notable. With them the history of the American people has been inseparably linked for about thirty years.

But I have never been able to detect that in any of them the Colonel greatly differed from the friendly, companionable, irrepressively high-spirited, and contagiously humorous young man who, during that autumn visit at Mandan, would co-operate with me in amusing my sister's baby, while my sister set the table and helped prepare the meals. For it would be impossible to imagine anyone occupying great and conspicuous positions whose public and private lives were more

126

nearly identical than his; and much in his character and manner—his emphatic cordiality, his
phenomenal memory for faces and names, together with a dozen unimportant but pleasing
and gratifying personal details that went with
them; his enthusiastic thoughtfulness for people
with no possible claim on him—much of all this
which in public life was so often attributed to his
tact and shrewdness as a politician, his genius for
"never missing a trick," was simply a magical
quality he had been born with, a spontaneous,
effervescent quality, as inseparable from him on
a Dakota hillside, or at the dinner-table of an intimate friend as it was at a political convention
or a White House reception.

It was what, I sincerely believe, at the comparatively early age of sixty-one, killed him. Prolonged, genial insincerity is no doubt something
of a strain, but an unremitting and absolutely
sincere geniality is a far greater one. It is an
actual radiation of vitality, and the Colonel
would have found that over which to radiate his
vitality had he been marooned in solitude on a
desert island.

127

My sister had two great dogs—an Irish stag-
hound and an English greyhound—and while
Mr. Roosevelt's experience had already compre-
hended many varieties of hunting in the West,
he had never coursed for jack rabbits with
hounds, and on two mornings we took him out.
In a certain sense the sport was a quite hopelessly tame one, for, incredibly fleet as both the
dogs were, they had never in their lives achieved
a jack rabbit, and we secretly considered it most
unlikely that they ever would. At the critical
moment the rabbit invariably "doubled" and
while the dogs stumbled helplessly over their own
feet in their clumsy efforts to stop and turn,
gained enough ground for perfect safety until
the next time. But to these exhilarating gallops
among the pale, dun-coloured buttes in the
neighbourhood of the thriving town of Mandan,
Mr. Roosevelt undoubtedly brought as much
enthusiasm as he had ever brought to the difficult and dangerous tracking of a mountain goat,
or long afterwards took with him to the game
trails of Africa. No human being could have
displayed more sincerity, and it was the same

128

sincerity and abounding quality that he retained almost until the last.

Something about him on the first morning had restrained me from confessing that my hands were suffering almost unendurable agony from the cold. I had forgotten my gloves, and by the time my fingers began to ache, I had with the inexplicable shyness of boyhood decided not to mention the matter or ride back to get them. The sun was not high, and as in that part of the world the wind never ceases, I was soon in torture. My fingers were like ten lumps of frozen iron, the reins merely hung on them as on hooks, and I wondered how long one could possibly stand such pain without beginning to cry. But I resolved that if I fell off the horse in my misery, I would never tell what the matter was. I scarcely knew young Mr. Roosevelt then, but there was that about him which caused me to shrink from complaining of something for which there was no remedy, and I set my teeth and became dumb as well as numb. Riding along beside me, he suddenly inquired: "Aren't your hands cold without gloves? Mine are even with them. I have another pair in my pocket if you'd like some," and he jerked from somewhere in his coat a pair of thick, knitted gloves lined with soft, fleecy wool. Well, there may be a heaven somewhere, but should I go there, I greatly doubt if it will contain for me any surprises.

For years after that I scarcely ever saw Mr. Roosevelt. He passed through St. Paul now and then and several times came to our house for luncheon or dinner—occasions memorable for their gaiety, their mirthful pandemonium, but it did not occur to me that he could take the slightest interest in me, for I merely sat listening to and enjoying the exciting conversation. My surprise, therefore, was great when after four or five desperately lonely weeks as a Western freshman at Harvard, during which I had literally talked with nobody except my landlady, there was a knock at my door one afternoon and a gigantic boy with an intensely strong, interesting face and a shock of dark hair exclaimed as he came into the room: "Hello! You know Theodore Roosevelt, don't you? Well, my name is Lodge and he asked me to come and see you—

130

the man's always doing things like that. I told him I hadn't the slightest desire to make your acquaintance, but he said to come anyhow, and here I am." Whereupon began for me a friendship with my class-mate George Cabot Lodge, the Senator's eldest son—a person of genius—which even his sudden death nine years ago does not seem to me to have in any essential manner ended.

Just as in public Colonel Roosevelt, without in the least intending to, constantly imparted to commonplace words and long-known phrases a new force and a picturesque charm that brought them instantly into current and widely popular use, in private life the same immense vitality and characteristic emphasis of enunciation caused certain purely conversational statements and ordinary turns of speech to become never forgotten household words. There is probably not a family that ever knew him without incorporating into its vernacular half a dozen of his volcanic utterances, not in the least because of their intrinsic meaning, but because of the manner in which he gave them finality.

The exclamation "I'm very sorry to hear it" is in itself scarcely an unusual one, but employed by the Colonel with a flash of teeth and all six words widely separated and emphasized, it became a thing apart, a cherished delightful thing, to be used with one's family only under very special circumstances.

Some twenty years ago he shot it at me upon my telling him that I had just finished reading some books by Henry James. "I'm verry sorrry to hear it" took on a colour, a vigour, a sincerity, and a reality that, until then, it had simply never possessed. Since then we have all, from time to time, used it among ourselves with an attempt at the devastating accents he put upon it, and it will always mean something it never quite meant before.

HOTEL DE LA GRILLE

A DAY or so ago I spent an hour with a friend who was sick enough to be in bed, but not too sick to talk and discuss and laugh. He had been last spring and summer in France, and as this six or seven months' sojourn was his first European experience, some of the things he said about it struck me as having a freshness of point of view, a valuable attitude of comparison and contrast, that I myself am somehow no longer able to command. For I was taken to Europe at the age of eight, was hauled all over it for more than a year, and have kept returning to it whenever I could. On one occasion I remained for a year, and the next time I went into the hands of a receiver and had to sail for home at the end of two extremely memorable weeks.

Our lives are made up of an infinite number of trivial details, and, somewhat unfortunately for literary purposes, I have come to take the trivial details of Europe too much for granted.

Much of the interest and perhaps the importance of living consists in being agitated, but the difference between living in Belgium and France and in our amazing land does not, I regret to say, any longer agitate me in the least. It did not, either, agitate my sick friend. He is a singularly detached, reflective, non-partisan citizen of the world, and it occurred to me that there was considerable compensation for having weathered half a century (as heaven alone knows how we both have!) when you can talk and discuss, state, expound, and describe without passionately taking sides or giving a damn, one way or the other. This is precisely what, for an agreeable hour, we did.

Without any question, in mechanical aids to progressing through the vale America is unrivalled. Our nice open-work plumbing, our "350 rooms, every one with bath," our white enamelled and porcelain civilization has its moments. Far be it from me to belittle them. There are times when I am really enamoured of my bathroom, with its elaborately conceived facilities, its fireplace, its atmosphere, combined of hygiene and comfort. Yet, when you get down to

134

fundamentals, do we not entirely too much preen and pride ourselves over these purchasable externals? They are, after all, merely expensive timesavers and vanities. All told, and in the end, they do not accomplish anything whatever that cannot be accomplished without them. I have recently been for eight months in France and Belgium and, except for one reckless and delirious week at Carcassonne, I never saw a "room and bath"; but because bringing-up and maybe temperament have inclined me to prefer cleanliness to squalor, I nevertheless maintained about the same standard, although not in the same painless and usual way. My friend recalled that in Paris there was a bathing-establishment some half-dozen doors from his rooming-house. To this he was accustomed to repair in his dressing-gown, pyjamas, and bedroom slippers.

In our country, he undoubtedly would have been, at best, criticized or, at worst, arrested. In Paris no one paid the slightest attention to him. His costume was not conventional, but in every respect it was quite as decent as trousers or skirts,

and the Parisian, tolerant and cosmopolitan to a
degree of which we in this "nation of villagers"
have no conception or understanding, glanced at
him, no doubt, and then was amused by an Arab
chieftain, an Indian rajah in a bejewelled turban,
an American soldier on leave from Germany, a
kinky-haired, dusky scion of one of the best families of Brazil, Raymond Duncan in Greek robes,
sandals, and not fanatically clean feet—or any
other of the countless exotic, surprising, thought-
compelling persons who are to be seen in the
Paris streets at every hour of the day and night.

"One always hears that living is more economical over there," my friend declared, "and so, in a
way, it undoubtedly is. But think of the things
you abandon."

"Yes, I agree with you," I replied. "But are
the things which we abandon the fundamental
things? Aren't they, after all, the extraneous
things—the prodigal, generous, on the whole
wasteful things on which so many of us have
grown to believe quite idiotically, in my opinion,
that we are dependent?" And we proceeded to
discuss the matter of illumination.

136

In every bedroom I have recently occupied in France there have been just two electric light bulbs except, of course, in the village inns where I have been so happy to stay, and where there often is no electric light at all, but it has never been possible to have both of these bulbs performing at the same time. If one is alive, the other is dead. It is most carefully arranged, and furthermore at half past midnight or one or two o'clock, as the case may be, they often cut off your electric light entirely. They assume, arbitrarily, and ridiculously, that after midnight, or one A.M., everybody ought to be down and out. As this seldom happens to be the case, you are sometimes, when you desire to read or to write letters at the pleasant hours most conducive to reading and writing letters, helpless and in despair. Personally I never am, because I have long been in the habit of storing away, in my travelling luggage, several packages of candles. They have been immensely useful in Mexico during the spring earthquakes, when electric light is often suddenly extinguished and does not return for several days. They are useful, too, in Europe,

137

where, in theory, you are supposed to have little frills like heat and light, but which, for economical reasons, have always been grudgingly furnished. The constitutional European stinginess in the matter of light never bothers me, because I was brought up on it. When I first went to Europe, there was in one's bedroom never any light except the glimmer of one or, at the most extravagant, two candles, and the curious, utterly un-American result has been that I enjoy candle-light, that I always have seven candles on my dinner-table, and that at night I often read myself to sleep by the light of two candles when, near by, a much more brilliant and efficient electric bulb would instantly respond to the touch of a finger.

With two candles one can read very nicely, and all the rest of the room—and the world, for that matter—is excluded, eliminated, banished. In some of the country hotels on one's way to southern France they still after dinner solemnly present you with a candle with which you uncertainly puzzle your way up the winding staircase to your clammy ten-acre room. But, as I

138

said to my friend, I never feel that candles are an imposition; I am accustomed to them, like them, and often prefer them.

Then, in amusing detail, he told me about his hotel in Paris and I replied with an account of mine—both of them; for I disliked the pretentious and rather unscrupulous little place in which I first sojourned and, after enduring it intermittently for six or eight weeks, acquired a large, airy, newly papered, painted, and upholstered room at fifty cents a day in a charming-looking, but also suspicious-looking, small rooming-house farther down the famous, narrow, and beautiful old street.

The first place took itself seriously; it served exceedingly bad meals, had several bathtubs that were perpetually out of commission, and an elevator that between the first floor and the fourth could make the stoutest heart quail, and turn the dyedest hair grey. You were supposed to memorize the directions affixed to the door of this engine of death and then, by pressing a series of buttons, hoist yourself upward. But, after dropping with the most unlooked-for and frightful suddenness into some sort of sewer the first time I got in and pressed a button, I never repeated the adventure without a chaperon.

"I'm afraid of this thing, and that's all there is to it," I explained one night to the clerk who was escorting me.

"But, sir, you need not be," he answered. "Yesterday morning I was stuck for an hour and a half between two floors and received not the slightest harm. I assure you—it is absolutely safe."

Then, too, the fat, blonde she-devil who conducted the place, although she did not own it, would never furnish me with a table or a desk to write on. Daily I besought her, pleaded with her, wrung my hands and lost my temper with her, while she merely looked fatter, blonder, and more pleasantly and maddeningly devilish than ever. The proprietor, she would declare, had gone to the country; on his return she would communicate to him my desire; without doubt the matter would be satisfactorily arranged. But weeks went by, the proprietor never returned from the country, literature languished and

died, and when from time to time I had to notify
my family that I was still extant or write a letter
of business, I achieved the act, occasionally on the
window-sill, now and then on the floor, sometimes with the aid of the top of my trunk.

Revenge, however, forthcame, and it was
worth waiting for. Late one night, on returning from the theatre, rather than invite fate by
attempting the elevator, I began to climb the
four interminable flights of stairs, and on floor
two, in the hall in front of somebody's door, was
one of the most agreeable-looking little Louis
something-or-other writing desks I have ever
seen. Without hesitation I picked it up and, like
the young man in the first chapter of Daudet's
Sappho, carried it in my arms to my bedroom.

The next morning the hotel was in an uproar.
A frightful, an unbelievable thing had happened—a valuable piece of furniture, a genuine
antique piece, had disappeared into thin air, had
been spirited away without a trace. The blonde
devil become apoplectic and I used to linger
shamelessly near her desk just for the joy of hearing her berate the mystified chambermaids. By

way of emphasizing her remarks on the occurrence she one afternoon slapped a chambermaid's face and was subsequently sued for assault or battery or whatever it is that chambermaids sue you for when you slap them. In the meanwhile I had a perfectly good desk, wrote endless letters and two chapters of a book, which, later on, I lost. I do not seem to remember anything about them now except that they were perfectly charming and that American literature has suffered an irrevocable blow.

To the day of my departure the secret of the miraculous evaporation of the Louis something-or-other writing desk was not disclosed. Luck happened to be with me; my chambermaid had arrived from the provinces the day on which I had committed the great crime. She naturally assumed that the desk had always been in my room. The poor dear knew no better and did not betray me. But oh, the concentrated venom, the "words," the face-slapping! I gloated over it and stayed on for three days longer than I intended to, hoping against hope that the blonde devil would come to an abrupt end. But she

142

didn't and I resumed life farther down where the rue de l'Université becomes the rue Jacob, in the suspicious-looking and charming bed-house that calls itself the Hotel de la Grille. From the first the Hotel de la Grille had fascinated me because, through some architectural aberration, it was not flush with the street; it stood three stories high, twenty feet back, and the intervening space had been turned into a kind of courtyard adorned with neatly clipped orange-trees in green boxes. At the sidewalk, there was a gigantic iron fence (the "grille" in fact) with a massive gate that Monsieur in some mysterious fashion was able, without stirring from the conjugal couch, to open for you when you returned at any unseemly hour. You always then shut it with a magnificent slam and on your way upstairs called out: "C'est moi—Flandrau. Bonne nuit, monsieur et madame."

About this queer little hostelry of only fifteen rooms (my acquaintances in Paris, after first considering me demented for living there, gradually acquired for the place an almost affectionate interest) there were two surprising features.

143

One was its dazzling cleanliness, and the other was its well-nigh austere respectability. I had not exactly expected either, and miraculously it turned out to be both. Monsieur and Madame were the most united and domestic persons imaginable, and Henriette, the only servant—a fragile, nicely blondined and hand-painted little creature who, without assistance, kept all the fifteen rooms in perfect order and carried large trunks up and down stairs with a song on her vermilion lips—was virtue and religion personified.

Monsieur had a taste for interior decoration and in a leisurely way and all by himself was gradually "doing the place over." A sort of inner courtyard was perpetually clogged with senile chairs, busted lounges, rickety tables, and rusty mantelpiece clocks that had stopped telling the time when Napoleon went to St. Helena. All day long he painted and varnished, upholstered, polished, and quite marvellously rejuvenated this junk, and we used to have interminable heart-to-hearts on the subject of wall paper. He would ask my advice and then dislike it when I gave it. The room he had decided to make a symphony in

144

blue I, for some perverse reason, longed to see a bower of passionate pink. He favoured papers with stripes because they made the ceilings seem higher. I inclined to all-over designs because they seemed to give the room a certain coziness. He conceded that I was greatly gifted with a "sense of style," but it was not French style, "and, after all, this is France," he would affirm.

In the room below me two middle-aged British spinsters vaguely studied art of some kind and, next door, lodged someone's young chauffeur who, in the street perpetually parked a series of ravishing limousines, touring cars, coupés and sedans. Above me was a personage out of Dickens. One morning when I asked Henriette where I could have some clothes pressed, she said: "Take them to the Englishman who resides over your head; he does very good work," and assuming that he was perhaps some young British valet temporarily out of a job, I knocked at the door.

A white-haired, vivacious man of eighty received me, and as we were almost at once sympathetic, he told me that while he had been born in London he had spent the first fifty-five

145

years of his life in Brooklyn. On the death of his father, who had been a tailor before him, he had returned to England and pursued his trade.

"But I always wanted to see what France was like, and ten years ago I came over here and have just stayed on ever since," he explained. "My room here is very comfortable" (he slept, tailored and breakfasted in it) "and although I have never advertised, I have more to do than I can attend to. Once I did have a hundred cards printed, but I distributed only about twenty. The other eighty are put away somewhere. One person seems to tell another. I'm worked to death because I hate so to disappoint anybody. This room, of course, is wonderfully comfortable and inexpensive, but I look forward to having two or three rooms. I miss my piano and my microscope."

Lulu, a nondescript spaniel belonging to Monsieur and Madame "had" twelve years. Fifi, however, who was owned by the handsome old lady, with a crippled daughter who conducted a newspaper kiosk in the courtyard "had" seventeen years and, while greatly beloved in the quar-

146

ter, was a delicate problem. Before I came to know Fifi well, I once indiscreetly stooped down and patted her aged, rat-and-tan back. It instantly brought on a "crise de nerfs." Fifi proceeded to have a temporary stroke of paralysis and was restored only after great difficulty with applications of ice and injections of strychnine. Returning from a sojourn in Belgium and not seeing Fifi around I inquired after her health. Bursting into tears her owner exclaimed: "Our little darling has left us forever. Last Wednesday she fell into a sleep from which we were unable to awaken her."

MELODEONS AND HOOP SKIRTS

THE reading room and the museum of the
Minnesota State Historical Society are oases of
quiet in a world of noise. If they have a fault, it
is probably that their meditative calm tends to
lessen one's belief in the urgency and importance
of whatever business has taken one to them. It
is a disastrous place to visit in a hurry, for over
the perfect St. Paulite (or should it be St. Paul-
ist?) it exercises an inescapable spell.

I confess that the removal of Little Crow's
scalp from a show case in the museum (where a
few years ago, some of his visiting Carlisle edu-
cated descendants were shocked to find it) to the
tactful seclusion of the vault, occasions in me a
pang almost as of nostalgia. The last time I saw
this startling yet profoundly characteristic me-
mento of our early history, the late Major Hol-
comb who, for many years unofficially at least,
did the honors in the Society's rooms, led me to a
dim chamber, closed the door, unlocked the
vault, and extracted all that was left of Little

Crow from a cardboard bonnet box. He ought not to have done it, of course, and admitted it, but he immediately added, and with some truth perhaps:

"Oh, well—what's a Sioux's scalp more or less between old settlers!"

But it was not Little Crow who drew me one day to the building of the Historical Society and persuaded me to remain there for several hours, when I had planned to leave without fail in fifteen minutes. Primarily it was the location of "Mazourka Hall." I had recently received a prettily printed invitation to a series of parties to be given at Mazourka Hall "during the present winter," and I wanted to find out just where "Mazourka Hall" was, or rather had been. For spotlessly white as was the invitation's satin-finished, gilt-edged paper "the present winter" was the winter of 1850, and my hosts had long since withdrawn from the activities of this earth.

The mazourka, no doubt, was one of the most fashionable of dances in the 1850's, and the hall in which St. Paul's larger social gathering took place was named in its honor. It stood on West

Third Street on the left-hand side of the Exchange street steps as you go down—at least, they say it did. First-hand information of St. Paul sixty-eight years ago presents certain difficulties. Naming the place Mazourka Hall was as thoroughly in the spirit of the times as not long since it would have been to name a similar place the Tango or the Fox Trot. Likewise in the spirit of the times was a phrase in the invitation's wording. The evenings on which the parties took place had been changed to Thursday, from some other evening and the managers of the series call attention not merely to a change of evening, but with infinitely more elegance to a change in "the period of their occurrence."

Did Mazourka Hall lose its vogue? It would seem so, for six years later "The pleasure of your company is requested at an Anniversary Ball, to be given at the Winslow House on Friday evening, the 22nd of February, 1856," and the Winslow House was at Seven Corners on the corner of Third Street and the Fort Road. This was without any doubt an occasion of splendor, for among the managers of the ball appear the names

150

of a governor, an ex-governor and many others
all unconsciously engaged at the time in making
local history, as well as several officers of the regular army stationed at Fort Snelling—to say
nothing of the Honorable Joseph Rolette and the
Baron de Freudenrich of whom I can discover
merely that "he said he was a Swiss." However,
any kind of a baron must have struck an interesting cosmopolitan note in the parlors of the
Winslow House, just as the Honorable Joe Rolette
in his half-breed costume de gala—heavily beaded
buckskin pants, beaded moccasins, and a frock
coat elaborately trimmed with dark brown fur
(it may all be seen in the Historical Society's
museum)—must have, entirely unaided, trans-
formed any gathering however would-be conventional into the romantically picturesque.

There were some twenty-five or thirty on the
managing committee, my father among them,
and perhaps, after all, the ball was gay rather
than only grand, for in 1856 Governors Ramsey
and Gorman were but forty-one and forty, my
father twenty-six, some of the others twenty-
two and three. No one was decrepit, exactly.

In the quiet reading rooms of the Historical Society one bygone event lures you irresistibly on to another, and long after I should have torn myself away to affairs more contemporaneous, I found myself deep in the locally brilliant winter of 1864-65, when the scenes of music, drama, philanthropy and the dance had once more shifted, this time to Ingersoll Hall on Bridge Square, the Atheneum on the corner of Exchange and Sherman streets, and Mackubin's Block, with three entrances, on Third, Fourth and Washington streets, respectively. It was in Mackubin's Block that the "Sanitary Fair" was held—a method evidently popular throughout the North at the time, of raising money with which to supply various comforts to the soldiers of the Northern army. It lasted four days, was by far the most ambitious co-operative effort the town had ever made, and cleared between thirteen and fourteen thousand dollars. Very delightful it is to read the many columns devoted to the event—long before, during and after it in the St. Paul *Press*—to note, among a multitude of other quaint items, that a special train would be run daily to and from Anoka, and that the crowds were advised by the paper to patronize as far as possible the Fourth Street entrance to Mackubin's Block as "the stairway being very broad, this is the best adapted for crinoline." It was an unusual, arduous and highly successful affair into which the whole population entered with enthusiasm, but I rejoice in the uncommon frankness with which, when it was at last over, the St. Paul *Press* editorially remarked: "Though the work was cheerfully prosecuted, every one was relieved at the conclusion of the Sanitary Fair."

Governor Miller donated the colonel's sword and sash that had been presented to him by the non-commissioned officers of the Seventh Minnesota regiment, recommending in his letter to the managers of the Fair that it be placed in the hands of some Minnesota officers below the rank of major or brigadier general "who shall, during the continuance of the Fair, receive the greatest number of votes accompanied by fifty cents each." He also presented "one hundred steel plate engravings of the present executive of

Minnesota" as he expressed it, modestly refraining from alluding to them by the more personal "myself."

General Grant also helped the undertaking with a letter of encouragement and appreciation expressed with his accustomed simplicity and common sense. "The season of the year selected for your Fair, and the high latitude of your home, will enable you to appreciate better the wants of our soldiers," he wrote; "although in a climate far milder than that of St. Paul, still our troops are operating in latitudes visited by frosts and snows."

Together with the invitations to the more strictly social events of the 1850's, two interesting programs repose on the desk before me, programs of entertainments given in connection with the Sanitary Fair, but at the Atheneum. One was "A Grand Tableau and Musical Entertainment"; the other "A Grand Tableau and Dramatic Entertainment," and they throw, both of them, some pleasant light on the period's taste in literature and music. The names of the participants were not printed, but a clever and charming woman among the audience supplied them in her own handwriting on reaching home after the performance, and also added some comments of a discriminating character for the benefit of a friend who was at the time visiting in the East.

Respect for the dead, as well as fear of the living, stays my fluent pen at this precise juncture, but it is perhaps not indiscreet after all these years to record that on the first program, under the printed item "Refreshments" she wrote: "A most sublime sell—quantities of sour oysters and spoiled dresses. Everybody lost temper and money. I hope experience will benefit them." In which connection the St. Paul *Press* the following morning admitted that "The only thing to be regretted was that the refreshment room was not more commodious."

"The Fair is over tonight" the same charming woman has also scribbled on the second program. "I'm nearly dead and ache from the crown of my head to the soles of my feet. The receipts were over thirteen thousand dollars—a tremendous success! Governor Miller's pictures (the steel plate engravings evidently) fell from fifty cents each, down to being retailed from the fish pond at five cents a bite!"

Scott, Dickens, Thomas Moore and Charles Reade seemed in those days to furnish the popular material for short dramatic scenes as well as subjects for living pictures. For *Guy Mannering, The Heart of Midlothian, Oliver Twist, Lalla Rookh,* and *Peg Woffington* were all in one way or the other represented. There was also "The Vision" from *Faust,* a "Joan of Arc," a "Coronation of Josephine," an "Arrest of Lady Jane Gray" and "The Huguenot Lovers" which last (so writes the dramatic critic of the St. Paul *Press*—a humorous devil like all of his horrid profession) drew from one of the audience the remark that "they did not appear much different from Americans."

Then, too, there was living statuary—"Niobe," Palmer's "Faith," "Praying Samuel," and truly up-to-the-minute "Zenobia." For the celebrated American sculptress, Harriet Hosmer, happened to be in this country for the moment, and "Zenobia in Chains," the newest example of

156

her art, at present in the Metropolitan Museum, was everywhere, among the cultured, creating much comment. Quite flawlessly in keeping with the period was a criticism of this statue in the enterprising St. Paul *Press*, a period in which an almost daily advertisement in the paper was "Melodeons and Hoop Skirts at Cost"; advertisements which sought to take the inherent curse from the melodeons by calling them "La Petite Organ" and by brazenly declaring that "to some extent it unites the powers of the piano with those of the church organ, while its capacity for the fit expression of sacred and home music, to which Americans are chiefly attached, is entirely superior to that of the Piano Forte."

"Womanhood," declares Miss Hosmer's critic who was unquestionably married and didn't care who knew it, "has made such wonderful progress during the last half century in our Republic— the type of that class of female representative of power has so intellectualized and has become so much more exalted and distinct as to need a different emblem for its beauty. The American ideal is more spiritual, more ethereally graceful

157

—slighter and less tangibly sensuous—than this majestic Persian.

"Miss Hosmer's own visit to her native country is a brief one. She sails in the *Persia* on the 17th to return to her studio in Rome, wedding herself, we are authentically informed, to single destiny of art. There is a sisterhood of such celibates of genius by which the world is thus robbed of a development—for we do not believe that this Zenobia is half what it would have been with the additional breathing of a self-felt passion. There will be more mere work, perhaps, to come from the virgin hand, but of voluptuous abandonment of inspiration there will be far less. Miss Emma Stebbins of New York is another of this sisterhood of genius and she also has taken up her abode in Italy—maiden, and gifted."

How perfectly it all chimes with "Melodeons and Hoop Skirts at Cost" and the fact that most of the music at the two entertainments we have glanced at was by Donizetti.

OF EARTHQUAKES

"They say," but with what truth I know not,
that the occasional person who has been born
blind and later on restored to sight is at first
somewhat inexplicably disappointed. And it is
not (so we are told) because the sense of sight,
as he imagined it, was of such a superior quality
to the quality of sight as it actually is, but merely
because the imagined quality was so absolutely
different. Very few of us have a gift for an-
ticipating actuality. An active imagination, of
course, scares up no end of things, but they unfortunately do not often turn out to be the right
things. With Morse and Edison, Marconi, Lord
Lister, Harvey, Pasteur, Roentgen, Sir James
Simpson, Mme. Curie, and people like that, the
matter is quite different. Their imagination indulged in what, at the time, appeared to be the
most preposterous excursions; but they happened
to be the kind of persons endowed with something akin to the faculty of divination. They
had a tolerably accurate idea of what certain

phenomena would be like should they, indeed, ever be induced to exhibit themselves and perform at all; and when finally, they got the things going, their unbelievable fantasies turned out to be just facts that no one else had forestalled. To mankind in general, however, it has not been given to realize the experience until it happens— an elementary axiom, the truth and force of which I had never in the least appreciated until, some six or seven years ago, I, for the first time, both experienced and realized an earthquake. It came over me then, when the planet had resumed its customary reserve (which it did after three or four indescribably horrible seconds) that sensation is something that simply can never be accurately imagined in advance.

Just as the blind, no doubt, conceive of vision, anybody can conceive of a good, husky, well-equipped, adult, businesslike earthquake. But in neither case can the conception have much in common with the thing itself. If a person has not experienced an earthquake, I discovered, nothing else that he has ever experienced will in any way qualify him even to recognize the sensation when it for the first time suddenly and dreadfully occurs. While my first earthquake was taking place, it never entered my head that something serious was happening to the planet; I was merely convinced that something frightful, and no doubt final, was happening to me.

We were having a cup of tea one April afternoon with some American friends on the little piazza of their house in Jalapa, Mexico, and the fact that their cottage was in the outskirts, almost in the country, seemed to invest what so briefly happened with an added mystery and horror. For about the locality there was almost always a rather blissful, rural silence. Across the street was the drowsy rose garden of an old English lady, and on another corner of the crossroads was an isolated "cantina"—a sort of last chance saloon—whose patrons right merrily shot and stabbed one another on feast days and Sundays, but which at other times seemed, in its deserted emptiness, to add to the general tranquillity.

All at once, in my low wicker chair, I had, while in the middle of a sentence, a feeling that

161

can only be described as one of complete mental and physical confusion. I forgot what I was saying, and my arms and legs, my entire body in fact, suddenly struck me as having become sickeningly incoherent. Incoherent is an absurd word to choose, perhaps, but since then I have sat through four or five Mexican earthquakes, and exactly that word has always occurred to me. I had in my hands a cup and saucer, and what flashed through my mind I am able, in all veracity, even after more than half a dozen years, to record, because when I got back to my room in the Gran Hotel, I wrote it down, and just now I have looked at what I wrote.

"This," I told myself, "is what is called a 'stroke,' apoplexy—paralysis. Well, anyhow, I'm glad it didn't happen in the street. Now I must put this cup and saucer back on the teatray before losing consciousness." By this time I was half out of the chair, and heavily, helplessly—back in it; and everybody was laughing and talking all at once; "Un temblor!" "Que temblor!" "Gracias a Dios—ya está!" and a great deal more in both Spanish and English. But

all around us was the same sun-drenched quietude
—the same damp, drowsy, undisturbed calm. A
most terrifying and awful thing had happened,
and yet, apparently, nothing whatever had happened. In the twinkling of an eye my entire
world had undergone an undreamed of, an altogether ghastly change; yet in doing so there had
been nothing visible, audible, smellable, or touch-
able to account for it. In fact, it has always
seemed to me to be quite impossible to determine
with any particular accuracy just which of one's
senses an earthquake reacts upon. We have only
a certain number of senses, and we of course have
to depend upon them to register. But an earthquake, or at least a first earthquake, has a way
of calling into exercise a kind of latent and
hitherto unsuspected sense—a composite, that
just for a moment or so leaves you with a desire to
cry a little and laugh a little, a slight, disgusting
nausea, and a curious terror which, you tell yourself, must be silly, not to say ridiculous, because
of the fact that it has for the time being established itself in the joints of your knees. On the
way back I recall saying to my brother, "Now

163

that I know what it was, I'm not a bit scared in my mind any more; but I'm still uncontrollably afraid in my knees." Between the time I had begun to feel frantically queer, and had been thrown back again into my chair, I had done quite a lot of thinking and planning, and the duration of the seismic disturbance, we discovered later, was between three and four seconds.

A week afterwards, at half-past nine at night, there was another. I do not desire any further testimony to the effect that we are wonderfully and fearfully made, that in the midst of life we are in death, that truth is stranger than fiction, that it is the unexpected which always happens, or any of those familiar sayings. They are all perfectly true, and never shall I dispute them.

The Gran Hotel is built about a courtyard, with a fountain in the centre, and innumerable plants and flowers stiffly arranged in pots and tins and tubs on the four sides all around it. Now, although I feel more at home in the thoroughly uncomfortable Gran Hotel of Jalapa than I do anywhere else except on Pleasant Avenue, I am obliged to admit that during the day this courtyard is one of the most bleak and unsympathetic spots in the whole world. It is scrupulously clean. Mozos spend the entire morning scouring its tiles, and the wife of Don Enrique, the proprietor, never lets a day go by without picking off every dried leaf and faded petal of the plants and flowers in the pots, tins and tubs.

Like all prosperous Mexican interiors, it is quite hideously clean, definite, bright, hard, and lacking in sympathy. During the day I have for long rather hated it, but after nightfall, I have always really loved it. For there are two arc-lamps, hanging overhead, and upon it the light that never was on land or sea—a beautiful, theatrical, artificial moonlight that transforms the place into a mysterious fairyland, in which exist only the lovely ghosts of flowers, the shadows of great moths, and the faint plashing of cool water. The bedrooms all open on the upper gallery that overlooks it and before going to bed I have always stood awhile, peering down into the entrancing falseness of it, and listening, sometimes to the fountain, and sometimes to the proprietor's wife playing on her costly grand piano the only "piece" she has ever learned, which with an appropriateness that, to me, has always seemed divine, happens to be the gifted Mlle. Chaminade's "La Lisonjera." To learning "La Lisonjera" she has devoted an hour or more a day for years, and she plays the thing remarkably well. But how perfect that, in the first place, she should have chosen something so pretty and dainty, so musically shallow and clever, heartless and delightful, theatrical and effective as a "piece" by Mlle. Chaminade! As nothing else possibly could, it accords with the fictitious moonlight, the riot of phantom blossoms, the twitter of a fountain. Nobody has ever skimmed, and then distilled, the froth of human sentiment with such delicacy, fancy and tact, as has Mlle. Chaminade. But I seem to be digressing. . . . What really concerns me for the moment is earthquakes.

Three ladies from Yucatan joined me in listening to "La Lisonjera" and gazing over the rail into the courtyard's wraithlike beauties. Then they excused themselves, saying that before retiring for the night they had planned to wash their hair. When Mexican women haven't anything else to do, they invariably employ the time in washing their long, blue-black hair, and as they almost never have anything whatever to do, their hair receives the greater part of their attention. In country hotels they come to meals with a bath towel affixed with safety pins to their shoulder blades, and their luxuriant tresses reposing dankly down the middle of it. It was difficult to bear at first—but in Mexico one learns both to ignore and to appreciate a lot of things. We parted—they to their dermatology, and I to the perusal, in my bedroom, of an American magazine I had got hold of which contained a short story by Mary Heaton Vorse, called "Teeth."

Never since then have I seen or heard of Mrs. Vorse's story called "Teeth" but it struck me that evening as being one of the most genuinely humorous—really side-splitting tales I have ever read; and I have often wondered how such a spontaneously mirth-begetting narrative could continue to remain hidden in an out-of-date number of a magazine. Over the bare, kitchen-like table in my ascetic tiled and whitewashed bedroom was a hanging incandescent bulb, and when I was about half-way through the story it all at once began to "do things." First, it swayed, to and fro, then it undertook a circular motion, and by the time I had tried to get out of my chair, and been plumped back again on it, it was spinning around and around overhead in great and ever-increasing circles.

By that time my "incoherence" was extreme, and I was distinctly sick at my stomach, but I wasn't in the least scared, because from the first, utterly loathsome sensation I had known what the matter was. I remember noting that through the nauseating silence (Oh, what a relief it would be if there were only loud and exciting explosions of some sort!) the great bell in one of the cathedral towers two blocks away, solemnly and portentously struck. Afterward it was said that it struck twice, once when the tower leaned, heaven only knows how many degrees from the perpendicular, and again, when marvellously, instead of toppling over, it righted itself. Very likely it did strike twice, but I heard only the one, fateful resonance; and then the bulb overhead went out.

The electricity of Jalapa emanates from a pretty waterfall in the environs of the distant village of Coatopec; in coming to Jalapa it passes over a graceful bridge which the earthquake with a slight twist of the wrist had neatly tied into a bow knot. All over Jalapa walls and roofs were collapsing and killing people and nobody could tell what was happening because a sudden velvet blackness had blotted it all out.

For a time, the only light in the world seemed to come from the candle I had groped for in my bag. Mexican electric light plants are more than ordinarily temperamental, and in some hotels the current is disconnected for economy, at midnight; so I was in the habit of providing myself with an unfailing supply of candles and matches.

Outside on the gallery overlooking the courtyard, the three ladies from Yucatan fell upon me and my little beacon with piercing screams. One of them fainted, and I have a most distorted recollection of keeping the candle lighted and at the same time helping to carry her downstairs and into the street, while the other two clung to me and moaned, and we were all more or less

169

suffocated and asphyxiated and drowned together in coils and ropes and hanks of wet, black hair reeking with soapsuds.

Once in the street, the only lights were the policemen's little mediaeval tin lanterns. Stumbling over people who, everywhere, were on their knees praying, I finally arrived at the Plaza—a nice, unencumbered space, where, unless the earth actually opened and swallowed one, nothing in particular could happen. Here, to my amazement, I discovered that through it all I had somehow clung to the magazine I had been reading when the appalling incident had begun. So, after awhile I borrowed the lantern from a policeman I happened to know, and sitting on a cast-iron bench in the Plaza I finished reading "Teeth," which must be one of the funniest stories ever written, because while I was doing this, canvas-covered litters with the dead and injured were being constantly borne into the Municipal Palace near by, and I laughed uproariously the while.

The next day, for the first and only time in my life, I wrote to an author I had not met.

170

HELLO! HELLO!

WITH the exception of a single numeral my telephone call is exactly the same as that of one of our leading florists, and in the dim, distant, nearly-forgotten period before our town had a really memorable telephone strike, when people wanted to buy flowers, my house was called up by mistake only two or three times a day.

Now, however, when the service is almost normal, it happens two or three times an hour, which is very annoying to those in quest of bouquets, and somewhat disturbing to me, who exist only to receive them. As a rule they begin by asking, "Is this Lemke's?" To which I politely answer, "No, it isn't" and this, for fifteen or twenty minutes ends the matter. By that time somebody else wants to buy flowers, and as no one at present in charge of the central switchboard has learned to tell the difference between two and three, I am then rung up again. It occasionally happens that the prospective purchasers do not begin by asking if I am the florist,

171

and as I am under no obligations to tell the story of my life every time the telephone bell rings, we sometimes have quite long and interesting conversations before they finally lose their tempers and hang up in a frenzy.

Yesterday morning, for instance, a lady started off by stating emphatically what she wanted, without first taking the precaution of finding out whether or not she was applying at the right place, and we communed somewhat as follows:

Female Voice: I want to order some flowers for a funeral, but I don't want anything very expensive.

C. M. F.: Flowers are terribly expensive just now, aren't they?

Female Voice: Oh, everything's expensive, but I just have to send something.

C. M. F.: It's the high cost of dying that really hurts, isn't it? Now let me see. Roses are ten dollars a dozen. They come all the way from Chicago.

Female Voice: Well, I won't send roses.

C. M. F.: Perhaps the deceased was not, after all, very near and dear?

F. V. (with asperity): I'm sure I don't see what that has to do with it.

C. M. F.: As a rule it has a good deal. Where there is genuine affection people don't seem to bother much about expense. Possibly this was just a connection by marriage.

F. V.: It was not. He was a business acquaintance of my husband's. I never even saw him. But we've got to send something. What is there cheaper than roses—a good deal cheaper?

C. M. F.: Well, there are always carnations.

F. V.: Oh, I never did care for carnations!

C. M. F.: Maybe he did though. Do you suppose there's any way of finding out? The personal touch is everything in these matters, and if you can combine exactly the right thing with the least expense . . . . You'll pardon my crude way of expressing it—I know you'll understand.

F. V.: Y-e-s-s-s-s, of course. But I simply don't like carnations. They look cheap.

C. M. F.: They are cheap. But a florist who really knows his business can wire them in such a way that with a few ferns, and three-quarters of a yard of inexpensive chiffon, they stick up

173

and look as if there were about four times as many as there really are. Unless you actually count them you'd never know. Then, too, if you wait until the very last moment before sending them, they probably won't be counted. The family will be too busy getting dressed.

F. V.: Young man, you talk too much.

C. M. F.: I beg your pardon, madam, I'm very sorry. I'm afraid I forgot myself.

F. V.: You certainly did. Now I want to know what you have besides roses and carnations. I may decide on the carnations after all. But I want to know what else you have first.

C. M. F.: How about some kind of a device? Had you thought about a device of some kind?

F. V.: No, I hadn't. Are they very expensive?

C. M. F.: Not necessarily. Sometimes quite small ones attract a great deal of attention.

F. V.: I'm not sure about a device. My husband didn't say anything about that sort of thing. What would you suggest?

C. M. F.: Well, of course, there are a great many different kinds. About the most successful one I recall at the moment—successful, that is to say, in the sense of occasioning comment—was a little rocking-chair made of lilies of the valley, with "Vacant" printed across the back in violets. As the man to whom it had been sent had weighed, when in life, 270 pounds, you can readily imagine that those present . . . .

F. V. (furiously) : I think this is perfectly outrageous—I've never been waited on this way in my life . . . (a great light suddenly dawns), Who is this, anyhow? I don't believe it's Lemke's at all!

C. M. F.: No, dearie, it isn't.

F. V.: Well, of all the . . . .

Bing!

"THE OLD THINGS"

Nowadays, very likely, little boys have more cultivated and uplifting tastes, but there was a time when almost all little boys, in this part of the world, at least, used to collect "tobacco tags" —small, metal emblems, stars, battle-axes, liberty bells, arrowheads and so on that were removed from various kinds of plug tobacco and dropped on the sidewalk by men who "chewed."

Since those distant days when we used to roam the downtown streets with our eyes staring at every inch of the wooden sidewalks, I have never collected anything. Much to my regret the good fairy who bestows upon people the collector's instinct was not present at my birth. Those who possess it are greatly to be envied no matter what form it takes, for it is as inexhaustible a source of interest and pleasure to the person who, only at rare intervals, can afford to buy anything, as it was to the late J. P. Morgan, who, with no intervals at all, was able to buy everything.

Acquisitiveness, however, was unfortunately

almost entirely omitted from me, and therefore it has always been a mystery to me why, while I was waiting for a street car at Seven Corners, some eight years ago, I should have gone into a second-hand store full of dilapidated stoves and chairs and lamps, and bought two large oil portraits hanging on the wall, and lugged them home with me. But, strange as it may seem, I did. They were both so dirty that one almost had to guess at their being the portraits of a man and a woman, and their ugly frames—of a much later date than the portraits themselves—were so large and heavy that the conductor at first refused them the hospitality of the back platform.

I paid a dollar for the two of them, wondering as I did so why on earth I should wish to possess the likenesses of two persons of whom I had never heard and for which I had no place. I have never found out; but at the present moment they are both glancing mildly at me from the floor where they have been leaning against the wall ever since the afternoon, eight years ago, when, at considerable inconvenience to myself, I brought them home.

177

A sponge bath of lukewarm water and castile soap did wonders for them. It revealed the fact that they were a nice-looking young couple who sometime during the 1830's or 40's had dressed in their best and sat to an artist of considerable skill. One feels that the man's likeness, in particular, was a good one. The dark blue dress coat and brass buttons, the high, rolling collar, the plaited shirt, elaborate stock and long, carefully combed up "pompadour" at the present time draw attention to themselves as a "costume," but the face itself, in its practical, unimaginative, rather narrow fashion is cleverly painted and very much alive. It is not an especially endearing visage but it has strength and intelligence.

His wife—one feels sure it is his wife—is not as well painted. I doubt if she was really pretty, but the artist felt under obligation to make her so, and in the process eliminated most everything in the way of expression except a ladylike simper. Her coiffure is Japanese in its intricacy, and it positively glitters with pomatum. In her hand (the painter was careless about hands) she holds

178

some pansies and small "thousand leaf" pink roses, and I have always been convinced that the diaphanous lace scarf about her neck was an afterthought of her husband's. For while the cut of her dress is primly modest, it does show an inch or two more than the most circumspect persons of a more elegant generation cared to reveal. I reconstruct the husband as saying to the artist: "In thinking the matter over, and before accepting the portraits, which are otherwise quite satisfactory, I feel that a slight suggestion of drapery just here, might serve to forestall any comment of a nature likely to inflict—you see what I mean." Whereupon the artist dabbed it on as quickly and unrealistically as possible.

When I acquired these two, I did not ask the proprietor of the second-hand shop who they were, because they were so obscured by the dirt of many years that it was impossible to see them well enough to care. But after they emerged in all their pleasant old-time finery, I returned to Seven Corners and tried to learn something about them. They had come from a boarding house on Cedar Street, but they had been there when the occupants of the place had taken possession. Who they were no one knew. The proprietor of the store had not wanted them particularly, but they were thrown in with the rest of the things. They had been hanging on his wall for about a year.

Since then I have been hopefully waiting for some one to turn pale while talking to me about the weather, and after controlling his (or her) emotion, to exclaim brokenly: "My great-grandparents! For forty years I have sought them far and wide, high and low, hither and yon. At last, at last. Name your own price." But no one as yet has.

I am not especially sentimental about this decorous pair, but I have grown to like them during the eight years we have lived together and I often think about them. Their fate has been that of nearly everything in the world which is not of sufficient practical use to be worn out, or sufficiently valueless to be deliberately destroyed. Portraits by the million eventually lose their identity, but it seems odd when they lose it so comparatively soon. It may have been

180

that the originals of these two had no direct descendants, but even so, very few persons of their
age are entirely unattached. Undoubtedly the
paintings descended for a time, and then either
the family died out, or all interest in them died
out. No, not quite all; for some reason I am at
a loss to explain, mine at least was sufficient to
cause me to part with a dollar, carry them home
and refresh them with a bath.

The fact that anyone did so is a curious little
tribute both to art, and, in a way, humanity.
As far as I am concerned they would still be
hanging above the stoves at Seven Corners if they
had been landscapes represented with the same
degree of skill. Of no practical value, and utterly forgotten as personalities or even as
branches of a family tree, they owe their continued existence entirely to their somewhat vague
connection with art and the human race.

The boarding-house keeper may not have
paused to analyze the matter, and very likely his
boarders hated the couple in the way boarders,
as a rule, do hate their temporary æsthetic en-
vironment. But the portraits survived notwith-

standing. It would have been easy enough to eliminate them forever in about five minutes, but nobody acted on such an impulse if it occurred.

At present my two unknown acquaintances are enjoying the shelter of an unostentatious Christian home. But, at best, it is a temporary asylum, and one speculates as to where they will eventually end. Time and again thoughts of the same kind have come over me in front of those fabulously expensive shops in New York and Paris, in which fine old family portraits, beautifully designed and executed pieces of furniture, silver and glass and chinaware, bits of jewelry and lace, temporarily rest from their mission of adorning somebody's home. Hundreds of years old some of them, they have seen the beginning, the rise, the progress, the decline and disappearance of families innumerable. Periodically have they found their way back to an antique shop or auction room and then, after a brief respite from intimate domesticity, have begun all over again with an wholly different set of people, as a wedding-, Christmas-, or birthday-present, or as

182

"the very thing we've been looking for, dear. Isn't it lucky we happened to stop and see it?"

In the history of any one of them there are half a dozen novels as absorbing as any ever written. They whet the curiosity by their silent eloquence on the mutability of "earthly grandeur" —the vanity of wishes. How well established, how solid and united must have felt the families who, in the first place, owned and used things of this kind! In imagination they saw coming after them a never-ending procession of descendants to whom such evidences of ancestral prosperity would be sacred relics. And now, not so long afterwards as time is computed, they are in a Fifth Avenue window waiting for somebody— anybody—to come along with the price.

Almost everybody at one time or another picks up or in some way acquires a possession or so that while not necessarily in the least valuable will nevertheless probably continue to exist until destroyed by accident. In my room, along with the lady and gentleman who came to me by way of Seven Corners there are, for instance, several objects of but little intrinsic value that I feel

sure have a chance to continue in the world long
after they have left my own affectionate possession. No one probably would destroy the small
Egyptian mummy case which, after fifteen hundred or two thousand years in a tomb at Luxor
now peers inscrutably into the future from my
mantelpiece. I got it up the Nile the day it was
taken from its long resting place, and although
thirty years of Minnesota have done more to fade
its blue and yellow and red decorations than did
two thousand years of Egypt, it is perfectly preserved and impressively mysterious.

It is doubtful, too, if anyone would be so
heartless as to make way with old Jacob Frede-
rico Torlade Peireira D'Azambuja, although it is
difficult to conceive of anybody whose importance to the world is less than that of the old
gentleman who, a hundred years ago, was minister to the United States from Portugal.

His house in Washington—or rather in
Georgetown, for at that time very few persons
actually lived in Washington—was next door to
my grandfather's, and one New Year's morning
he came to call and presented the family with a

large engraving of himself in his diplomatic uniform with three orders as large as saucers on his left chest. Under it his many virtues were described in florid and unblushingly complimentary Latin. Probably no one in the world but me would have the slightest idea who this pleasantly pompous old creature was, but, somehow, I can't believe he will be wantonly destroyed.

Near by is an almost painfully gay little work which on closer examination proves to represent the hanging of thirty-eight Indians at Mankato in 1862. Certainly no one could ever wish to destroy that—a charming bit of color, aside from its historical interest. And not far away, by a most happy coincidence is the large, firm signature of a well-known personage who was not hanged but beheaded. In 1786 a cousin of ours —an army officer—was spending some time in France with his wife and child, and this was their passport permitting them to travel and leave the country, signed "Louis Par Le Roy." The signatures of kings will doubtless be spared because they will probably soon be so rare.

RAG BAG

WRITING, when you come to think of it, is really a strange sort of occupation for an able-bodied person to be engaged in. At times I have even rather despised it. In detached and cold-blooded moments it has often seemed to me to be a performance both silly and useless, and more than once have I definitely resolved to acquire a few of those undulating acres across the High Bridge, along what used to be known as the Dodd Road, and with their aid achieve a certain poise and dignity by causing potatoes, cabbages and onions to grow where none had grown before.

But now and then writing—even my own— strikes me as being wholly justified. For some curious reason I have always been helplessly dependent on the writing of others—even on the writing of those who haven't nearly as much facility and skill in the matter as I have myself. Why should this be? Quite clearly, I see that sometimes they have neither felt nor grasped their subjects, and that in treating them they display no particular aptitudes in the way of logic, observation, beauty, either spiritual or verbal; and yet I read them.

Why, then, on precisely the same principle, shouldn't some one read me? For all I know he may. One thing is certain. All over the world have I been abjectly grateful to persons of whom I have never heard and shall never see, who have spent part of their time in crocheting and knitting with words and then sending the result to the printer. The mere fact of being alive has always seemed to me to be an extremely dubious blessing, but in connection with this painful reality, there have arisen many alleviations, among which, most prominently, stands out the printed page.

Biologically speaking, the two most urgent impulses of the human race are the impulse to eat, and the impulse to reproduce itself, but with a great many persons—many more than is usually realized—the impulse to read (just to read—anything—everything) is almost as imperative.

Last summer a vivid, breezy and distinctly young man of about sixty described to me an

187

experience he had gone through while reluctantly making a visit, and the episode seems to have lingered in my rag-bag mind as significant and illustrative of what I have just said. He had been transported by his charming wife to spend three days at Newport; an adventure he invariably dreaded, but one he had for many years been obliged at stated, and stately intervals, to undergo. In the hurry of departure he had forgotten to take along anything to read, and he said that when he finally adjourned to his Louis Seize bedroom, which was very beautifully and authentically furnished with some of the chairs, sofas and tapestries that poor, dear Marie Antoinette herself had actually enjoyed, he all at once realized that he wasn't in the least sleepy and that he had absolutely nothing to read.

"It may seem trivial and unimportant to you," he declared to me, "but I give you my word, to me it was terrible—tragic. For the first time in my life I had some idea of what it is to be a dope fiend deprived of his dope. I craved to read. I should have fallen upon the bosom of the telephone book with a scream of relief; but in per-

188

fectly appointed Louis Seize bedrooms they don't have telephones, and the fascinating books that go with them. I got into bed. It seemed to be the only thing to do, but I couldn't sleep. Before I go to bed I always read and read, and without it I was wretched. Finally I got up, put on a dressing-gown and, fumbling for electric switches, gradually made my way down to the magnificent mausoleum they called the library. On its shelves there were some hundreds of thousands of dollars' worth of books—folio Shakespeares, and all that sort of thing, I suppose—but they were all covered with glass and locked up.

"While I was trying to pry open one of these literary coffins, a footman, in pyjamas, appeared, brandishing a revolver. I said to him, 'My boy, if I can't get something to read, I think I shall die.' To which he pleasantly replied: 'Oh, don't say that, sir. In my room I have the *Police Gazette*, *Snifty Stories*, and *Tom Toothpicks*. They are at your disposal. Will they not tide you over—serve their purpose?' And the wonderful part of it," so declared my informant, "is, that somehow, they marvellously did."

189

The impulse to read is queer enough, but the impulse to write strikes me as being much more so. At the present moment, for example, I am most placidly anchored in the shabby old room that, with the exception of nine years, has been my exclusive property ever since I was born. The curtains are drawn, the fire is making gentle, companionable overtures, the green-shaded lamp from time to time sympathetically breathes. In the midst of this dear, if dusty paradise, why does not one just contentedly exist? Inexplicably, one doesn't. Instead, one seizes a pencil and endeavours to communicate—with whom it doesn't particularly matter. There is both the desire to say things, and to say them with a certain neatness. It is unaccountable. You are aware that no one really cares, and yet you begin, and keep on and on. To me, the great impediment in the way of writing is not that there are so few things to write about, but that there are so confusingly many.

Just now, for example, all sorts of things are crowding up, insisting, begging to be talked about. The subject of restaurants asks to be exploited. There is a whole, long chapter eventually to be written that in minute detail will differentiate between dining, and merely eating. Some people eat, and others have an odd, no doubt perverted, effete, languid, incorrigible yearning to dine. They like to do it slowly, artistically, climactically.

For some reason they themselves could not very well explain, they wish to have perfect things perfectly presented to them. I have never been tenaciously attached to the hodge-podge of habits to which we flatteringly apply the term "civilization." But given the term—accepting it for what it is supposed to mean—I have long cherished a theory that so-called "civilization" begins at the precise moment at which people leave off merely "eating" and begin to "dine." This, of course, amounts to a verdict to the effect that most human beings, judged even by their own, low standards are uncivilized. Well, they are. One would like at length to go into this matter, and investigate the difference between just filling a vacuum, and administering to the trained and fastidious senses. Personally, I have

191

a tendency to consume sardines and gulp tea from the edge of a kitchen table, but none the less I am acutely aware that there is a different procedure for which there is much to be said.

Interior decoration is another topic on which with ever so little encouragement I feel it in me to become not only eloquent but metaphysical. After an interval of about thirty-five years, I've got around to having some house-cleaning done. Kind but firm young creatures in white garments are performing complicated surgical operations on my walls, and it's all very distressing. But what I should like to investigate and follow up, is just why one picks out, and decides upon, one type of wall paper rather than another. In the various rooms there is a lot of hideous furniture that, so a clever professional female tells me, needs but a coat or two of grey or ivory paint, and a dab or so of color to make it all "perfectly lovely."

Well, I have girded my loins, set my teeth, and embarked on the adventure of coating and dabbing; but why? In the end, the furniture itself will perform exactly the same functions it has always performed. Why this superficial but nerve-racking transformation? I don't know. It ought to be thought about, and then at length written out and explained. No doubt it is a human groping toward the harmonious, the beautiful—the ideal. In camouflaging a Grand Rapids bureau of a very bad period, I shouldn't be surprised if one really, in a way, was seeking God. Don't laugh—I mean it! How else can you explain the yearning, effort and expense? It's an awful bureau, but eventually I'm going to make it a better bureau, a beautiful bureau— a beatific bureau. Why does one do that? Some day I hope to fathom it, and then sit down and try to make it plain.

Very much also do I wish to write about running a garage. It is a tremendous subject—more potential, even, than interior decorating and restaurants. By accident I have in the past seven months come to learn a great deal about the garage business, and it is of surpassing human interest. Nowadays the "garage" man occupies something of the place of the "confidente" of the French classic drama. In spite of himself he is the intermediary, the go-between, the repository. He has, in a surprising degree, usurped the less technical functions of the old-time, historical manicure, hairdresser, and seamstress. Sooner or later he comes to know everything about everybody, and there is about everybody a quite incredible amount to know. As far as I am aware, no one has deeply delved into the garage man's possibilities, and I long to cast some light upon them. He has, all in the day's work, the most electrifying tales to tell on the subjects of domesticity, finance, alcohol and the affections. He has become a clearing house of the world's scandal, not necessarily because he is that kind of a person, but because, somehow, it just happens. On the garage business I have, from time to time, been taking a few notes, and later on I am, with as much thoroughness as is humanly possible, going to make them public. If I have never been pursued before, I certainly shall be, then. There is so much to write about. The chief difficulty consists in shutting the door

upon the insistent multitudes that come crowding, hinting and imploring to be noticed, and
commented upon.   A single essay is too small—
a single life, too short.

THE GUIGNOL, REVISITED

OF the many interesting aspects of children, to me at least, the most interesting has long been the fact that they can be "brought up" only once. There is nothing irrevocable about becoming engaged, getting married, building a house, entering a business or a profession—embarking, in fact, on many quite important human ventures. Some persons become engaged at least once every summer for years, and in this country it has long been easy to get rid of a husband or a wife if for any reason, however trivial, he or she does not suit. Women frequently have been known to invest in new husbands because the old ones didn't take them often enough to the movies; men have exchanged inconsiderate wives who refused to fire up the kitchen stove at five A.M. for the true, helpful, womanly type of woman who would. Rebuilding a house or buying a different one is merely a matter of having some money and a capricious mind, and as for the professions, almost anybody can recall a

196

number of excellent clergymen who started as something else, or half a dozen lawyers who evaded the penitentiary by the simple method of becoming eminent statesmen.

If at first you don't succeed, try, try again, does not, however, apply to the bringing up of children; at least not to the same children. For when it is once done, it is done; and the responsibility involved occasionally strikes one who has no children and consequently no responsibility in the matter as being little short of appalling.

Of course, as one is so often told, "you can get used to anything," and apparently most persons, with much facility, get used to parenthood. Naturally there must be a great deal of planning and methodizing and worry in connection with the relationship that to a bachelor never becomes apparent; he probably isn't told of it because it is, erroneously, supposed to be something in which he does not take any interest. But even so, to the uninitiated there often seems to be something amazingly casual in the manner in which so irrepealable an act as the bringing up

197

of children is performed. My own early years are those about which I am most intimately and thoroughly informed, but while I am deeply grateful for them and singularly at peace with them, I confess myself to be incapable of imagining and grasping the point of view of a parent with sufficient faith, hope and courage to have permitted them.

After many years, I look back on at least one of them with unending diversion, wonder, interest, curiosity. There was about it everything to remember with affection—nothing with regret; but in the abstract the entire idea of it now seems to be simply preposterous—the sort of idea that, in the event of my having children of my own, I could not under any circumstances for a moment maintain. Often in much later years, with a sort of awe, I asked my mother how she ever managed it, existed through it, and she admitted that the year and a half she had spent in Europe, with two children aged respectively eight and four, no nursemaid, and very little money, was the sort of adventure a mother indulges in just once; but she would usually add,

with what justification I do not know, "After
all, when you and your brother were eight and
four, you were in a good many respects about as
grown up as you ever will be."

It wasn't as if we had settled down in some
quiet village where there was little to see and
nothing to do but go to school, as we would have
been doing had we remained at home. Oh! dear,
no! Except for the better part of a winter in
Rome, and the spring and early summer in Paris,
we travelled incessantly, and if there is a picture,
a church, a historic site, a famous view, a sentimental or literary shrine of any kind that we did
not see, beginning with the British Isles and pursuing an indefatigable course through Belgium,
Holland, France, Italy, Switzerland, Germany,
Spain, Gibraltar, and even part of Morocco, it is
merely because Baedeker himself had neglected
to notice it. Thirty-eight years ago Spain was
anything but an easy country to travel in, especially for persons who could not speak Spanish,
but we investigated Spain from the Bay of Bis-
cay to the Gulf of Cadiz, part of the time on
mules. Anything that was undertaken at all had

to include us, partly because we refused to be left behind, and partly because there was never anyone with whom we could very well have been left.

The proceeding gave both my brother and me a familiarity with the commonplaces of existence in foreign parts that has never worn off. Both Europe and Mexico have since then seemed to us to be many things, but they have never seemed to us to be disconcertingly foreign. In Cadiz, I remember, my brother was sick in bed for three or four days with croup. He from time to time varied sudden and inopportune attacks of toothache with even more inopportune attacks of croup, and, of course, my mother had to take care of him night and day; but I didn't let the incident interfere with my seeing Cadiz. With a guidebook and enough money for cab fare, entrance fees and tips, I, at the age of eight, saw Cadiz, not thoroughly, perhaps, but sufficiently, and I remember much of it to this day.

In Paris, dear heaven! we used to be frequently taken at night to the Odéon and the Théâtre Français, not at all in a misguided effort at early education, but merely because if we had been left in bed at a hotel, or pension, the place would undoubtedly have chosen that particular evening on which to burn up, and nobody would have rescued us. We always at the theatre sat away upstairs somewhere, not only because it was cheap, but because it was inconspicuous. For my brother, who went to sleep as soon as we got comfortably settled in our seats, was in those days given to having a nightmare almost every evening at a quarter to ten, and when this happened during the third act of one of the French classics it invariably occasioned considerable comment on the part of the adjacent audience.

As a matter of fact, the Parisian pension in which we stayed longest did catch fire one afternoon, and by reason of the conflagration we were denied its further hospitality. For I set it on fire myself while making chocolate on an alcohol lamp. The curtains went first, and while my brother and I were discussing what, under the circumstances, we had better do, one of them fell off and set fire to a bed. After that, Madame did not quite see her way clear to continue the arrangement which, and so forth, and so forth.

It must have been terribly trying to my mother; we were always being put out of hotels, and for perfectly good reasons. In Edinburgh in one of those sepulchral, morgue-like, so-called "private" hostelries peculiar to Great Britain and mid-Victorian Philadelphia, we destroyed a highly valued tablecloth while trying to cut slices of bread with a sharp carving knife, and on the shortest and most inconvenient notice had to seek a roof elsewhere.

But in Paris, until I fired the pension and Madame fired us, the existence we led was an entrancing one, and although I cannot for a single instant picture myself as a parent taking the same line, there has always been to me something inestimably precious in the fact that there was once a parent who did.

The pension was in the rue Honoré de Balzac, a narrow street running at right angles from the upper end of the Champs Élysées, and every morning after breakfast my mother used to take us to the garden of the Tuilleries at the extreme other end of the great avenue and turn us loose for the day. It was really, when you pause to consider the matter, a rather extraordinary thing for a mother to do. Entirely alone, with not a human being to whom we could apply for advice or protection or any of the ministrations of which children are supposed to be so perpetually in need, we day after day amused and took care of ourselves in the roaring midst of Paris from about ten in the morning to four or five in the afternoon.

At that hour we were hunted up and taken home, until one afternoon we decided for some reason or other to seek the rue Balzac earlier and alone, and as we succeeded in navigating the vast expanse of the Place de la Concorde and ascending the mile or more of avenue without difficulty or mishap, we thereafter were allowed to go to and fro unattended whenever we felt like it.

In recent years few spots in the world have seemed to me so terrifying and impossible to traverse as the Place de la Concorde in the late afternoon. It is at least twenty times as bad as Fifth Avenue, because it is not only as crowded, it is twenty times as far across. Nothing would induce me to walk across it now, but at the age of eight and four we used to take each other by the hand and saunter in and out among the traffic without a second thought. There were, of course, no motors in those days, but the hundreds and hundreds of cabs were like a disturbed ant hill, and until the automobile arrived and added a new obstacle in the way of keeping alive, cabs, carriages and drays seemed just as much of a menace. But nothing ever happened to us and nothing that was not wholly delightful ever happened to us in the Tuilleries either.

We each had a hoop, a small, gaily painted tin pail and a spade, but why the pail and spade I do not know, for there has never been any place to dig in the Tuilleries. From end to end except where there are flower beds, its hard, flat surface is covered with fine gravel. However, French children at play always have a hoop, a pail and a spade, and we, after the manner of children the world over, had to observe the local convention. We used to join in the decorous games of the other children when their nurses and governesses would let us. Sometimes, indeed, they wouldn't but I cannot recall having felt hurt at the exclusion; there always seemed to be plenty of other things to do.

One of them, and by far the most never ending in its fascinations was the Guignol—the Punch and Judy theatre in the centre of the gardens that opened at one o'clock and continued its performance throughout the afternoon. It was a solid, permanent edifice, not the flimsy, portable Punch and Judy affair of other lands, and it had four complete sets of scenery, a large company of wooden-headed actors and a curtain that rolled up and down. In fact, it was in all these respects remarkably like grown-up theatres.

To attend the performance on a chair cost fifteen centimes and during the course of the afternoon we, to this extent, were extravagant and magnificent, just once. Among the three or four plays given we had a favorite, and when it became evident that it was about to be performed we bought tickets and sat in the front row where we could hear every word. Most of the time we stood free of charge behind a rope which separated the populace from the elect, but while one could see just as well, it was now and then difficult through the great surrounding unceasing Parisian roar to hear and understand. Seventeen years later I went again to the Guignol, hoping to stand once more behind the rope among the baker and butcher boys and the children who had already squandered their fifteen centimes on a favorite drama, and I had a sense of personal affront on discovering that the proprietors had spent the intervening seventeen years in growing, where on three sides the rope formerly had been stretched, an impenetrable hedge six or seven feet high. No more free Guignol; no more excuse for the messenger boys to tarry on the way, and no more would it have been possible to pass whole, happy afternoons there unless one had a pocket full of centimes.

The kiosk where "gaufres" were made was, however, still as easy of access as ever and I bought two waffles and near by a glass of milk and a roll, and sat down on a bench to consume them, as that is what we used to do by way of luncheon when we began to feel hungry. And when, after a little, it began to rain, I hurried out of the garden and under the arcade on the other side of the rue de Rivoli, for that is what we had always done when it rained. There was no place else to go, and besides, in the arcade not far from the gilded equesrian statue of Joan of Arc there was a most superlative toy shop. It was and is still there, its windows as alluring as ever. As I examined them it seemed to me that we really must have had a good deal of sense so many years before, for it came back to me that we had always deliberately saved the protected windows of the tiny shop for literally a rainy day. Even under the most adverse climatic conditions there was an unfailing resource.

I am sure that novels like the first parts of *Peter Ibbetson* and *Christopher,* dealing as they do with Anglo-Saxon children, in France, have for me a charm and a poignancy and a meaning that can be shared only by those who found out something of France at an age when they were not aware of the fact that they were finding out anything. But often, while I have been reading them, or while I have been trying

to picture my tiny brother and me wandering
back through the disturbingly golden, late afternoon light on the Champs Elysées, the affection
and gratitude for the memory is divided with un-
belief, amazement and mirth that such things
ever were or ever parentally could be.

P.S. A surprising number of years have now
unaccountably evaporated since my brother and I
first flattened our noses against the toy shop's
dazzling vitrines, and the place itself has undergone no change. While still obviously successful (it sells favors for the cotillon as well as toys)
it is exactly the same size and painted the same
yellow-brown mud-color. The dolls, however,
have answered the call of the age. Last year I
passed the beloved window almost every day for
four months, and by every law of nature I ought
to have been shocked on discovering that most
of the lady dolls had bobbed, hennaed hair,
plucked eyebrows and rouged cheeks—that they
sprawled on the shelves in attitudes of indescrib-
able abandon—that they wore form-fitting, one-
piece bathing suits, and that they one and all
smoked cigarettes.

THE COLT

THE United States has long been a "lawless" country, and it is becoming more lawless every year. One deplores this, of course, but one also partly understands why it should be so and often sympathizes with at least the impulse if not always with its manifestations. The insuperable obstacle in the way of American reform is the American reformer, for no enlightened and self-respecting American has, in his heart, anything but scorn and disgust for the professional reformer, and a more or less continuous emotion of scorn and disgust renders it always difficult and sometimes impossible to differentiate between the reformer and reform. Often openly, but more often secretly, enlightened and self-respecting Americans regard most Congressmen, most clergymen, all officials of the Y. M. C. A., and all professional reformers merely as so much human vermin.

One of these meddlesome Matties or busy Lizzies (if you prefer rhyme to alliteration) snooping around my back fence not long ago, observed on my premises a hoofed quadruped of the genus Equus, more familiarly, perhaps, known as the caballus, and most familiarly known as the domestic horse. This particular example was of an extreme shagginess, but even beneath the abundant covering provided by an ever-adaptable nature against the rigors of a Minnesota winter, it was easy to detect that the horse was gaunt; not actually thin, but angular. The vertebra sagged; shoulders, hips, withers and hocks called to themselves undue attention. Undoubtedly there was something the matter with this horse. It didn't look in the least like the horses you see trotting along the streets. Horses that had enough to eat never looked like that. Well-fed horses were always plump and sprightly. Ah! A case for the Humane Society, perhaps (delicious possibility) even for the police!

A fiend in human form named Flandrau is maltreating and starving one of our four-footed friends in his back yard! Deliberately starving a horse! Quick—let us inform and reform! There is no time to lose. We mustn't stop or inquire and find out anything so prosaic and unessential as facts, and the amusing truth of the matter. We are reformers, and our business in life is to meddle first and find out by accident, later on. Inform upon him—bring him to justice! Almost no sooner said than done. Informed upon I was. Here is the, to me, wistful fact:

Some thirty-odd years ago I acquired for forty dollars in North Dakota a wild, beautiful little bay mare that I could not bring myself to part with, and eventually brought home. I rode her for a year, and it was a great grief to me when a slight accident to one of her hind legs developed blood poisoning, and she had to be shot. Before this happened, however, she had one morning, to our complete astonishment, miraculously appeared with a lanky male child who bore a startling resemblance to herself, and this unexpected gift of God I have ever since retained.

He is thirty-two years old, and is still referred to in the family circle as "the colt." I have always intended to give him a name, but time slips by so rapidly that I have never got around to it. Gaunt, grey, angular, beautifully venerable, he

211

is still "the colt" and no doubt always will be. He was brought up, not as a horse, but as a puppy or kitten. From the first he craved human companionship, as well as the sugar that somehow seemed to be inseparable from it, and from the day his mother died, he haunted the kitchen door. Not only did he haunt it, he soon, with a persistence and an amazing ingenuity he has ever since maintained and displayed, learned how to open it. With the combined resources of his teeth and his tongue he could, after a few trials, coax the china door knob of the kitchen door to revolve, and he would then, with his nose, push open the door and enter. As the cook loved him, much of his young life was spent in the kitchen. Once, I recall, he thrust his velvety little muzzle into a pan of rising dough, and not liking the result, he attempted to rub off the evidence of his indiscretion on a red-hot stove. It was all very sad. I had to sit up through several nights changing, from time to time, alleviating poultices.

As a rule, horses have to be what is known as "broken"—a masterful, dominating term, of immense support to human conceit, and I had a worried idea that when at last the colt's back was strong enough to bear me and a saddle, there would be much trouble. But not at all. The colt appeared to think it all right that I should pry open his mouth and insert into it a ridiculous metal implement, that I should affix a pad on his back, hoist myself upon it and set out to explore the world. From the beginning he was enthusiastic about it. He never objected to bit, saddle or me, and all over Minnesota we often had funny, even picaresque times. Thanks to the colt, I know certain parts of Minnesota with an intimacy it would be impossible now to attain. And always has he been a fascinating problem in heredity.

From his Indian mother, for instance, he has remembered that underneath the snow there is grass, and just as his maternal ancestors, on the Montana and Dakota prairies did before him, he still, in the back yard, although full of expensive food, paws up the snow and nibbles at the faded grass underneath. No truly civilized horse would do this. In a snowbound back yard any

213

civilized horse would just shiver and starve. Sustenance might be beneath his hoofs, but he wouldn't know how to go about getting it. The colt has always known. And furthermore, the colt has always known something else. His mother was a shy, wild little Indian woman who passed on to him the secret of pawing up the snow and finding grass underneath, but papa, whoever he may have been, was an equine highbrow, for the colt has always had, without even so much as a suggestion, as many gaits as a laboriously, tediously and distressingly instructed Kentucky thoroughbred. He must just have inherited them from his father, because with a twitch of the rein he has from the beginning, without hesitation, gone from one to the other —the useless, super-refined, little high-school frills that ordinarily are the result of such prolonged and relentless effort. He was born knowing them all. Papa's ethics were doubtless informal, but it is impossible to question his education. To his son he transmitted all sorts of motions and rhythms he himself had painfully acquired. Very likely half a dozen erudite scientists can be found to refute and rout me. But I can't be routed, for the colt's funny little, inherited, imitation gaits were the perpetual delight of my boyhood. Even now I think he could be induced to show them.

There came a time when he was no longer ridden, but he had a rather grand interval of being "hitched up" to a light vehicle and trotting about town on errands—to the grocer's and butcher's. He liked that. He felt terribly important. Every now and then he used to give evidence of a "gosh-darn-it-I-think-I'll-kick-out-the-dash-board-and-run-away" tendency, but he never actually carried it into effect, and while for many years he remained a proud, prancing and spirited little creature, he was at heart sedate and home-loving and respectable.

Certain rather Indian traits he still retains. Even now he occasionally plots and plans to sneak up on the dogs as they lie stretched in the sun, and ecstatically trample them into eternity while they sleep, but after he has worked it all out and proceeds to carry it into execution, the dogs, at the critical moment, are somehow never

215

within trampling distance. They have waked up, yawned, and moved away to somewhere else. It is disappointing, but hope springs eternal, and after an hour or so of more plotting and planning, he tries again, with always the same lack of results.

About fifteen or sixteen years ago his iron shoes were removed, and he has never had any new ones. His contacts with hard pavements were never prolonged, and they became more and more infrequent. For years now, he hasn't been out of the yard, and the safe, placid, meditative, philosophic existence he leads is second only to that of the cow. The two, indeed, are great friends, and I often wonder what they have in common. For it is evident on long, drowsy summer afternoons, when they stand close together, languidly switching at persistent flies with their respective tails, that, in some way, they communicate. It may be that the colt is extolling the virtues of sugar, and the cow is upholding the inestimable advantages of salt. They both are perpetually on the lookout for a chance to enjoy these dissipations, and whenever I ap-

216

pear, they excitedly make for me and prod at my pockets with their eager, clumsy noses. The colt's is like warm velvet, and the cow's—a wet and sticky nutmeg grater—is ruinous to one's clothes.

During a year or so the colt must have had, now and then, some vague, dim appreciation of the meaning of war, for there were times when his sugar was not forthcoming. Occasionally in order not to disappoint him, I would sweeten my coffee and tea with cane syrup (which as it happens, I liked just as well) and give him what I was entitled to use myself. He used to prefer it in lumps, but nowadays although he is still abundantly supplied with teeth that look like green tombstones, he likes it granulated and greatly enjoys making a little puddle in the palm of my hand and then dabbling in it with the end of his moist, smooth tongue.

He has plenty of teeth, but either they don't meet with the old-time accuracy, or they have become sensitive, for no longer is he able to consume hay as he used to. He selects a wisp of it, fletcherizes it for five or ten minutes and then, instead of swallowing it, abandons it—or, to be grossly accurate, spits it out. But none the less, his appetite is wondrously unimpaired. Of soft things, barley, corn-meal mush, and the more expensive grains, he consumes unbelievable quantities. And he thoroughly enjoys life. If he didn't, I long ago should have relieved him of the burden of it, but as yet, it has never been a burden. He has protracted, intimate discussions with the cow, makes daily and elaborate plans to annihilate the dogs, meditates and eats a great deal, and is on the whole happier than any one of my acquaintance. After thirty-two years, to a reforming eye he doubtless has lost some of his youthful beauty. He is angular and shaggy, and the hair of his dear old cheeks has become quite grey, but as long as he has the courage to enjoy this world of sorrow and sin, I shall let him do so. By the county assessor he is valued at nine dollars, and I pay taxes on him. Theoretically—technically—I am the pampered and luxurious possessor of a steed. The fact of itself automatically places me among the accursed rich, and yearly I pay for the privilege.

218

THE COLT

Just recently a reformer, like most reformers, panting, half-baked and idiotic, has reported me for cruelty to animals. Of reform there is always a crying need—but how instinctively one loathes vermin.

JARANA AT BREAKFAST

My brother and I were having breakfast, and in one corner of the large, bare room (the "sala," as it is magnificently called) where we ate, and sat, and spent most of our time indoors, the harpist and his son were discoursing wild and terrible music. They had played all night at a dance (oh, those Mexican country dances!), at a little coffee ranch near ours, and on the way home through the jungle, a mere trifle of fifteen or eighteen miles, it had occurred to the harpist, in his amiable drunkenness, to stop and play to us. In the saturated atmosphere of the tropics it is impossible for more than a few minutes at a time to keep any kind of a stringed instrument in tune, and the saturation of the player scarcely adds to its accuracy and general tone.

The son, a boy of fourteen, played the "jarana" and was perfectly sober, although after a night of hard work, the jarana did not sound so. The Spanish dictionary tells one that the meaning of "jarana" is a "merry clatter," but the

jarana of my acquaintance is a kind of home-
made guitar, ingeniously constructed from the
shell of an armadillo, and at breakfast, as an
obbligato to papa's savage bursts of drunken, Indian song, its clatter is not especially merry.
Every now and then this early morning concert
contained suspicions of a distinctly recognizable
tune, but at all times its syncopated rhythm was
marvellous, and its din was absolutely deafening.
We didn't attempt to talk, my brother and I.
With only the table between us, we were obliged
to shout and yell.

In the midst of this pandemonium, which to
us seemed entirely natural and commonplace, as
it had often happened before, there was a sudden rattle of hoofs on the tiles of the piazza, and
an exhausted American we had never seen was
lifted from his horse by the Mexican who had arrived with him on a mule. It was an amazing
thing to have happen, as the place for many
years was one of the most inaccessible in the
world, and on the very rare occasions when anyone, not a Mexican, contemplated coming to it,
we learned of the visit weeks, even months, in

advance, and then it usually did not take place. This wholly unexpected guest had been in the country just four days. He did not know a word of Spanish, he had never in his whole life been on a horse before, and after spending the better part of three of his four days on one, he introduced himself to us, quite seriously, with the information that he thought he was going to die.

He didn't, of course, but spent a week with us instead, at the end of which he was able to sit down and stand up without prolonged preliminaries such as setting his teeth, screwing up his face, and swearing, and we greatly enjoyed his companionship. It was particularly diverting to be present at the awakening of an intelligent and amusing compatriot who had, so to speak, gone to sleep in New York and next opened his eyes in Mexico at its most unrelievedly and remorselessly Mexican. For he had come by boat to Vera Cruz, taken the three-and-a-half-hour trip by train to Jalapa immediately on landing, spent a day there waiting for an eccentric brother who failed to meet him (his ranch was some fifty or sixty miles from ours), and then decided to start out and search for his brother alone.

To be exact, he was not alone, for he had with him the mozo on a mule. But as the two were unable to communicate with each other, and as this youth had not the slightest idea of the object of the expedition, he was valuable chiefly in taking care of the horse, and assisting our guest in his perilous and painful ascents and descents of it. After three days of almost impassable mud, swollen mountain streams, squalid Indian villages, a hair-raising drop of five thousand feet, which in a few hours translates you from a temperate climate to the wet, exhausting heat of the tropics, he had arrived at the little town of Mizantla, and, as there is nothing beyond Mizantla except thirty-five miles of burning sand dunes and the Gulf of Mexico, he had paused for the night.

Here, to his astonishment and delight, he had found an old Frenchman—a relic of the French occupation during the time of Maximilian—and, as he spoke a little French, he had been able to learn, among other things, that he had gone

223

some sixty miles out of his way, and that near by on a hillside in the jungle there lived two very strange Americans. "Near by" proved to be seven of the longest and most horrible miles of all, but, unable to sleep on account of the raw, sickening, strangulating smell of the vanilla beans that had been stored in his room at the dreadful little inn, he had started early and had discovered us breakfasting to the "merry" and deafening clatter of a jarana and a drunken harp.

Just one characteristic agony of the Mexican countryside he did not experience until he was almost within a stone's throw of our front door. His horse having stuck fast in the mud, he dismounted and sunk into it himself up to his knees. This, of course, had happened on his journey innumerable times before, but this morning he had pulled himself out by grasping, with his bare hands, a stout bush that grew in convenient luxuriance on the edge of the trail, and as it was the viciously poisonous plant called "mala mujer" (bad woman), by the time he reached the house, his hands had begun to swell, and for two days his pain, in addition to all his other pains, was truly excruciating.

Never, before or since, have I laughed so much as during the week he spent with us. For without some preliminary experience—a more gradual initiation than he had been given—no one had ever penetrated those wilds.

Not only were everything and everybody new to him; their newness was unbelievable, and over some of our entirely innocent and matter-of-fact remarks and conversation he had a way of, literally, throwing up his hands, rolling his eyes out of sight, and groaning: "No—no—no! Oh, please don't! You really mustn't!" In our excitement at his arrival, we had neglected to make any explanation of the music, which had lost all control of itself and couldn't stop. In fact, we practically forgot about it until he exclaimed with some annoyance: "Do you two always have this hell-raising with your breakfast? They said in Mizantla that you were Americans. I think myself that you are a couple of Irish kings."

A pig tied to the leg of the cot in which he had slept at the Indian village of San Juan Bau-

225

tista had been disconcerting; but the asphyxiating fumes of the vanilla beans in Mizantla were infinitely worse. More than once I had tried to sleep in that room myself and could sympathize with the nausea and dull headache it had given him. His constant amazement and incredulity were natural and entertaining to us, but one phrase that instinctively rose to his lips a dozen times a day, while understandable perhaps, was often irritating, implying, as it did, a wholly unjust criticism of ourselves.

"But why don't you change all that?" he would demand, when to his notice would be brought some typical and unreasonable Mexican trait with which we had struggled for years in vain. Deferential and gentle as everyone on the place appeared to be, it seemed to him merely a lack of energy on our part that stood in the way of revolutionizing Mexico's temperament, habits, and morals overnight. And here let us leave him, in futile impatience with the people's temperament, and aghast at their morals, to cite some characteristic manifestations of both.

Rosalia, the cook, washes our clothes, as well

as her own, by taking them to the brook, soaping them, and then pounding them on a rock with a wooden paddle. This makes them almost clean, and also removes or breaks such buttons as may have clung on by the skin of their remaining teeth since the time before. Returning to the house, she spreads everything out on some low weeds and coarse grass growing near by, and before they have had a chance to dry, twenty-five or thirty chickens and two ducks have strolled on them; half a dozen dogs have taken a short cut across them, and one of the mules, after making away with a sock and a handkerchief, begins to chew with sensuous abandon on the corner of a tablecloth.

About this time Rosalia discovers what is happening, as well as what has happened, and expresses both extreme surprise and deep concern. If she hasn't anything particular to do and is in the mood, she gathers all the clothes up again, repairs to the brook, and repeats the process of soaping and mutilation. But if she is occupied, or engaged in conversation, she merely chases the mule away and leaves the clothes lying on

the ground for a day, two days—three days—
until she gets round to washing them over again.
It is literally true that she has been known to
wash all the clothes three separate times before
she was able to rescue them comparatively free
from the footprints of dogs, ducks, and chickens.
But why don't we change all that by providing
Rosalia with a clothesline and kindly but firmly
requesting her to use it? Why not, indeed?

From the distant City of Mexico we have imported hanks of clothesline, coils of clothesline
—miles of clothesline; and, while many admirable and practical uses have eventually been
found for them they have never been used for
the drying of clothes. Rosalia has never seen or
heard of such a ridiculous and insulting device
and couldn't possibly undertake to employ it.
To do so would somehow amount to an admis-
sion of former carelessness, or a deficient knowledge of what is really what. She doesn't say
this, but her disparaging shrug conveys it.
Should one become kindly firm, Rosalia would,
first, protest that clotheslines were "not the custom of the country," and, second, acquire a

completely incapacitating headache. (I can see
her now with a large green leaf of some kind of
herb ostentatiously stuck on each temple.)
Should firmness be unwisely persisted in, she
would find by the following day that the climate
of that locality had never quite agreed with her,
and that she had never really intended to stay
that long anyhow. In short, Rosalia has never
used a clothesline and there is not, in the whole
world, money or power sufficient to persuade
her to use one. It simply can't be done, and that
is all there is to that. There has been a succession of Rosalias at my brother's place in the past
ten or twelve years, as well as a succession of
clothesline, but the former have never once
deigned to recognize the latter.

Ramon, my brother's "major-domo," as the
foreman on any Mexico farm, however small, is
grandly entitled, is a nice young country fellow
of about twenty-seven, whose family, like many
families in that part of Mexico, was given a few
acres of land generations ago and has lived on
them ever since. Ramon, together with his numerous brothers and sisters, came at first just

to pick coffee during the picking season; but as he could read and write as well as "figure," and as he rarely drank and was a serious, steady person, he was, greatly to his surprise, made majordomo. Ramon is honest and good, and he also has two wives. At the cost of about eight dollars apiece he has built each of them a bamboo house on our place, and each of them has several children—mostly Ramon's. One of them we are accustomed to refer to as "Ramon's wife," and the other is known to everybody as "Ramon's other wife," but just why the invidious distinction it would be difficult to say, as Ramon has never actually married either of them. He has not with either of them even had the religious ceremony performed in church. The religious ceremony in Mexico is neither legally valid nor necessarily binding, but as Ramon is economical (although one might not assume so) and not given to display, he omitted all formalities. Ramon is devoted to both his wives and exceedingly kind to them and all of their children, and, in spite (or perhaps because—I am not in the least sure) of his excessive domesticity, he is one

230

of the most highly respectable persons of my acquaintance anywhere.

But why don't we change all that? It is doubtless a most shocking and reprehensible state of affairs that, at my age and with my ethical advantages, I should have quickly grown accustomed to saying without a smile or a thought: "Good morning, Ramon. How is your wife? I trust your other wife is also as well as usual." But how could it have been otherwise? No one thinks the less of Ramon for supporting two families. Indeed, he is respected as a conscientious idealist; for with no loss of public esteem he could have abandoned both of them and gone to live with someone else.

The only really valid marriage ceremony in Mexico is the civil ceremony, but to a Mexican peon there is nothing interesting or emotional about signing a document in an office, so when he indulges in a ceremony at all he usually prefers the religious. This, however, is not binding, and he knows it, and the result is that the marriage tie is informal beyond belief. Couples live with each other as long as it is convenient, and no longer. Often, it is true, the convenience lasts till death; but even more often, especially among the young, it does not. There is considerable difficulty from year to year in knowing just who is who, and, of course, it is all wrong.

But it would be out of the question to begin to change matters by picking on poor, dear, respectable Ramon. He is sober and industrious, and both his little establishments are unusually well cared for and contented. He wouldn't in the least understand any point you could possibly make and would probably exclaim in deep perplexity: "But I would have to get rid of one of my families and they would have to go and live with somebody else—and they prefer me."

(¹)

THE END